handholding: 5 kinds
sonic, textual engagements

Kubrick
Akomfrah
Stein
Schwitters
Cage

Tracie Morris

KORE PRESS TUCSON 2016

Kore Press, Inc., Tucson, Arizona USA
Standing by women's words since 1993
korepress.org

Designed by Lisa Bowden and Drew Burk.
Set in Garamond and Meta.
Cover design by Sally Geier

We express gratitude to the National Endowment for
the Arts, the Tucson-Pima Arts Council, the Arizona
Commission on the Arts, and to individuals for
support to make this Kore Press publication possible.

Library of Congress
Cataloging-in-Publication Data
Morris, Tracie.
[Poems. Selections]
Handholding : 5 kinds / Tracie Morris.
  pages cm
ISBN 978-1-888553-91-8 (paperback)
I. Title.
PS3563.O87449A6 2015
811'.54--dc23
2015031256

Shylock: This is kind I offer...

Bassanio: This were kindness.

Shylock: This kindness will I show.

> —William Shakespeare's
> *Merchant of Venice*,
> Act One, Scene Three

Table of Contents

Foreword and Backward
Charles Bernstein

For the last two decades, Tracie Morris has been transfiguring the relation of text to performance and word to sound. Such iconic Morris works as "Slave Sho to Video (a.k.a. Black but Beautiful)" and "Chain Gang" are scoreless sound poems, originating in improvised live performance. At the same time, Morris has published text-based work in *Intermission* (1998) and *Rhyme Scheme* (2012). *Handholding* is the first collection of Morris' work to present a full spectrum of her approaches to poetry. This is not so much a collection of poems, as conventionally understood, as a display of the possibilities for poetry. Each work here is not just in a different style or form but rather explores different aspects of poetry as a medium: re-sounding, re-vising, resonating, re-calling, re-performing, re-imaginings. In *handholding* the medium is messaged so that troglodyte binaries like politics and aesthetics, original and translation, and oral and written go the way of Plato's cave by way of Niagara Falls.

In her first recordings, Morris was already crossing the Rubicon between spoken word and sound poetry, showing that the river was only skin deep. In one of the two revisionist versions of a major modernist poem in this collection, Morris returns to the magnum opus of modernist sound poetry, Kurt Schwitters's "Ursonate" (1922-1932). For "Resonatæ" Morris does not perform Schwitters's score; rather, she collaborates with the signal recording of the work by Schwitters' son Ernst. You don't hear Ernst's recording in Morris' work, but she is taking her cue from this performance. Because Morris has dispensed with the written (alphabetic) score, she is able to improvise, loop, extend, and re-perform "Ursonate" in a way that sets her performance apart. Her tempo is at half the pace of Christian Bök's magnificent, athletic version. "Resonatæ" re-spatializes the pitch of "Ursonate" as she re-forms its rhythms, creating a meditative, resonating, interior space that makes a stark contrast to Bök. While Bök's performance creates a concave acoustic space, Morris creates a convex one. This becomes especially poignant midway in the performance, when rather than create a percussive rhythm with phonemes popping against one another, Morris practically lapses into speech, into talking, into direct address. "Resonatæ" is a brilliant charm, deepening and extending this modernist classic in a way comparable to Glenn Gould's revisionist Bach.

"eyes wide shut: a not-neo-benshi read" is another thing entirely. This poem invents a new medium for poetry, based on recent adaption by some American poets of Japanese "benshi" (live narration for silent films). "eyes wide shut: a not-neo-benshi read" provides a new commentary track for the Stanley Kubrick movie: the audio file synchs with the full movie, while the printed poem is a sort of paratext or microfiche version. The two versions of the work are incommensurable; or maybe the relation is like a song lyric to a song. Listening to the audio track alone, the experience is of long silences, with voice suddenly breaking into the silence.

"Songs and Other Sevens," like "eyes wide shut," is a commentary on a movie, John Akomfrah's 1993 documentary, *Seven Songs for Malcolm X*. Morris again provides discrepant versions: one on the page, two as sound recordings. In this case, the audio is not meant to accompany the film but to provide a shadow version of the text (or perhaps it is the other way around and the text is the ghost of the audio). Listening to the audio tracks, the silences stand out as much as the sound in a way that undercuts the rhetorical momentum associated with poetry performance. Morris makes the space between the lines palpable. The neutrality of voice brings to mind the French poet Claude Royet-Journoud's desire for a lack of acoustic resonance in a reading (Royet-Journoud employs a timer to insert non-rhythmic silences between cut-up phrases). With this frame established, the alphabetic poem seems non-linear: you can read it backward or move around in it, sample it.

All that silence is made explicit by "5'05"," Morris' transcription/ transposition of the John Cage classic "4'33"," where Cage frames a silence that is filled with ambient sound as well as with the sound of listening. Morris records sound as space: rooms, which like stanzas, can be a place to breath or an enclosure that closes you off from the world.

"If I Re-viewed Her," Morris' reworking of Gertrude Stein's *Tender Buttons* (1914) is a textual tour-de-force and the perfect bookend to her Schwitters: two towering modernist classics startlingly transformed. Stein: thou art translated! There is some connection to Harryette Mullens' *Trimmings* or perhaps to say that *Trimmings* is a touchstone for what is done in "If I Re-viewed Her," Morris affords much cultural surround to her Stein variations and impromptus: Shakespeare and Williams, Yiddish and Broadway. She gives Stein back her accents, entering into a dialog with a work that veers toward soliloquy. Crucially, Morris re-sutures Stein's relation to blackness, which Stein was unable, given her time, to come to terms with: "What she said here is unfortunate. It isn't fortune and it isn't innate. I'll leave it there but it was a disappointment. I'll say that. (She won't.) A 'white old chat churner' after all."

In "If I Re-viewed Her" Morris asks the two central questions for *handholding*: "What's a room?" and "What's an heirloom?"

She doesn't show, she tells.

June 10, 2015

Preface

The genesis of this book begins with *Eyes Wide Shut*, the film by Stanley Kubrick. It jumpstarted this entire project. I have been fascinated with the film for over a decade and couldn't put my finger on why. (I'll say more about my relationship to the film in my introduction to the piece.) As my connection to it intensified, it seemed to "draw" like projects to it until I finally realized that I had a full book and not just the chapbook I originally intended.

Each of the pieces here has its own story, its own reason for why its presence in this collection. Most of the ideas generated here were written and inspired while I was on sabbatical from my home academic institution, Pratt Institute in Brooklyn, NY. The sabbatical gave me the headspace to travel and to bring these experimental pieces into light/life. (My travels in the US are represented in the ambient recordings of 5'05".)

The sound pieces are related to the page-based pieces but are also intended to stand alone. I've improvised in both media, so neither is "faithful" to the other. They can be experienced on their own terms. This is the first time that I've been interested in recording my speaking voice, reciting page-based work for one of my own books. I may not do it again but I just felt that it made sense here.

I want to thank Lisa Bowden and Kore Press for their patience as the manuscript grew and costs increased. I want to thank Jemman for advice with the cover. I want to very much thank Kelly Writers' House of the University of Pennsylvania and especially Al Filreis, Jessica Lowenthal, Kenneth Goldsmith, Zach Carduner with assistance from Kaitlin Moore of The Freddy Wexler Studio at KWH for making these incredibly clear recordings possible.

Many influences and confluences made this book come into being. Three artist colonies insured that the book was completed: I first began to experiment with Schwitters' work at the Millay Colony of the Arts in Austerlitz, New York, while teaching a workshop there in 2012. I completed the manuscript at Yaddo in Saratoga Springs, New York just before I left the retreat in 2015. I edited and recorded the sound files (with the obvious exceptions in the 5'05" section) at MacDowell Artist Colony in Peterborough, New Hampshire in 2015. I am also tremendously grateful for my time at the Abbey of Gethsemani in silent meditation. In some ways, I've come to realize that Thomas Merton's legacy in silence and in discourse with those outside of his way of life, is present in this work.

I am deeply grateful to these colonies and retreats for allowing me to cultivate this project as I was pursing my (other) primary work there. Each experience felt like a divine intervention. I'm also appreciative of my colleagues there who helped me to talk out some of these ideas and/or who stimulated them with their presence.

I thank you for getting this book and hope you find that it holds your interest and generates more interest in the great artists and their work that inspired mine. I hope, if not to measure up to their excellence, to demonstrate my sincere appreciation. I'm humbled to reflect upon them and am glad their work is in the world, waiting to be taken in.

How to Approach These Collaborations

Since this isn't exactly a conventional narrative progression/collection, I thought I'd make a brief note about the way I'm approaching these collaborations. You can, of course, do what you like, but below was the intention I had when I created them.

I hope you have moments when you can read along/listen along with me and Kubrick, Akomfrah, Stein and Schwitters and Cage. There are different media, genres and types of collaboration under the rubric of "handholding."

The first is to be watched/read (for Kubrick – please turn on the closed caption feature while watching) and heard simultaneously; another is to be heard and read (reading *Tender Buttons* and listening and/or reading both texts simultaneously as legal proofreaders do). You can watch along with the recitation of Akomfrah's *Seven Songs for Malcolm X* (while it's not required to understand the text it does further illuminate it). And lastly one is to be heard simultaneously (listening to Schwitters' "Ursonate" and "Resonatæ" together, but again, the text does exist on its own).

Of course you could just read this book without the other media, especially if you're familiar with the other texts (in particular the last one inspired by Cage's 4'33"). It's up to you. I hope you find them in either way/any way. Thanks again for picking this up.

About the Audio

Audio is accessible for listening or download at korepress.org/TracieMorris

Kubrick: *eyes wide shut:* a not neo-benshi read, 2:28:31
Akomfrah: Songs and Other Sevens 1, 13:41
Akomfrah: Songs and Other Sevens 2, 52:31
Stein: If I Re-viewed Her, 1:47:28
Schwitters: Resonatæ, 41:14
Cage: 5'05", 1:33

Eyes Wide Shut, Mouth Narrowly Open: An Introduction to a Conversation

I've been fascinated by Kubrick's work after seeing *2001: A Space Odyssey* as a nerdy, sci-fi loving child. I'd also seen his extraordinary work, *A Clockwork Orange* probably at too young an age. As kid and teenager, I had learned to find great satisfaction from artists who were great storytellers even if the end of the tale didn't result in unambiguously happy endings. My early exposure to the work of Edgar Allen Poe and Robert Cornier (author of the novel *The Chocolate War*) reinforced this predisposition.

When I first encountered *Eyes Wide Shut*, it was on my computer and at night. It was a personal experience with the film. I couldn't shake how unusual and intriguing it was. Over the course of the last ten years I've seen the film many, many times, dozens of times actually, and always find something new. However, I could never quite get to the bottom of why I was so intrigued by it, besides the excellence of the storytelling. I researched it, wrote notes about it and just kept the film hanging around inside my head for years.

Divine providence: I was asked to be on a panel for the annual Associated Writing Programs conference in 2013, held in Boston, for a panel called: "Feminism Meets Neo-Benshi: Movietelling Talks Back." I finally decided to wrestle with my love for this film. I was encouraged by Lisa Bowden at Kore Press to consider developing the project, as we had been discussing a collaboration for years. (We'd been introduced to each other by the wonderful Frances Sjoberg, during her tenure as Literary Director at the Poetry Center in Tucson, Arizona.)

I developed a talk-back for the first 10 minutes of the film. During the discussion, the poet and activist, Dr. Ching-In Chen, raised the important issue of cultural appropriation of the term "benshi." Before that discussion, I'd titled my effort: "*Eyes Wide Shut*: a neo-benshi read." After Ching-In's comments, I retitled it "*eyes wide shut*: a not-neo-benshi read." I wanted to acknowledge the connections that inspired this "play" and to respect Ching-in's correction. (I was also attracted to the notion of "talk back" as a phrase. The idea of talking back as the movie is playing, often with extensive commentary, is a well-known signifier of Black audiences watching films, both in public and in private. It's part of our call and response tradition from antiquity and applies to a Black presence through speech acts, the topic of another book I'm developing. I didn't include it in the title because I didn't want to feel that I was arguing with Kubrick, as many Black people do as part of our engagement with cinema.)

I'm interested in offering another "read" on the film. My ruminations on it, feminism, Ching-In's comment and the relative absence of Black presence in the film (as is also the case with Poe and Cornier) began to impact my interest and understanding of why I continued to sustain interest with this movie. I also noted that my friend Arthur Jafa, the renowned director and cinematographer, was involved in *Eyes Wide Shut* behind the scenes. We had briefly discussed it a long time ago and one of the things we remarked upon was why it wasn't more popular among our many arty friends.

The connections didn't stop with my feminist friends and Black friends (or the concentric circles of same), however. More good luck came my way when I happened upon an antiquarian shop in London, recommended by a friend of mine, Andrew Vivnevski, at The Royal Academy of Dramatic Art. I was working on yet another project in London (which is increasingly becoming the nexus of most, if not all, of my upcoming book projects) and saw a coffee table Kubrick book. I mentioned my interest to the son of the proprietor and he said that Kubrick's archives were in London. So I hopped on the Tube to see them. Fortunately, I hadn't quite sent in the manuscript to Lisa, Kore's publisher (who has the patience of Job) as I was considering adding two other portions on Stein and Schwitters that are now included in the book.

The Stanley Kubrick archives are meticulously and lovingly maintained by the excellent staff dedicated to special collections. Poring over old scripts, reference books, photos and other materials was extraordinary, yet somewhat manageable. (Thank goodness. If I'd decided to do research on my other two favorite Kubrick films I'd never have finished this book!) There was surprisingly little about the film, but what was available was thoroughly researched and catalogued so I could find exactly what I was interested in (mostly about the gender reversal of the role of the ingénue from female to male, or, "Bill Harford as Damsel").

One of the things I found there, as I was waiting for the boxes to be brought out, was a beautiful little meditation on the film by French theorist Michel Chion. I was so taken by the book that I wrote Mr. Chion and he was kind enough to write me back. I cannot hope that my small effort could be as wonderful and insightful as his work but he inspired me to try and not give up because Kubrick is rather intimidating and working with this extensive film is a formidable task. Mr. Chion enlightened me on a few ideas and confirmed some thoughts of my own that I thought were rather "out there." It's almost as if I found my literary mentor in this section of the project, despite the fact that I had already done two drafts of the piece and sustained firmly ensconced opinions about approaching the film before I encountered his work on it.

What all these wonderful coincidences reinforced was something I was trying to get at when I presented at the conference. "Just who is whom here?" What is the notion of identity and how does it play out in this strange tale?

There's a lovely line in Roberta Flack's song "Reverend Lee" that she speaks before she starts to sing about someone: "… who thinks that he has his program all together until he runs up against the lady who shows him that he *ain't* got it together…" (and of course, Reverend Lee encountered a demonic presence after a sexual experience, so there's that added reinforcement by the song).

Race plays a role in the film *Eyes Wide Shut*. Part of the Bill Harford breakdown at the end of the film, his complete emotional exposure to his wife, finally, has to do with his sense of White privilege. He feels secure in who he is, what his life means, because he's an affluent, straight, attractive, White, able-bodied male, with a beautiful wife in a privileged social position as an elite doctor. ("His name was Reverend *Doctor* Lee…"). By the end of the film, none of these aspects of his life protect him from the bursting of the bubble of the world he created for himself based on his naiveté.

This is epitomized in the specific casting of, and performance by, Tom Cruise. I'm deeply indebted to the Kubrick Archives for concretizing this fact for me. The original drafts of the script written by Frederick Raphael had a language and attitude that was much more like the New York that I grew up in and that Stanley Kubrick undoubtedly did. It was a mix of vivacious Black people, Jewish people, Latinos, Queer people,

Italians, Irish people with a discernable, specific New York accent. Not the neutral American Midwestern accent and repressed WASP affect that Cruise presented in the film. Raphael's language was also more relaxed and connected to the kind of discourse seen in "Rhapsody/Traumnovelle," the German book by Albert Schnitzler that inspired the film. The casting of Cruise, rather than say, a younger version of Sydney Pollack, offered contrasts that one otherwise would have missed. It also made other substitutions more likely by Kubrick (such as the substitution of homophobic aggression for anti-Semetic aggression in the original book). There were also overt Black casting choices in earlier versions of the script that were erased from later versions, such as the first lines of the script that specifically discuss "black slaves" in a children's book that Helena reads, the presence of a Black chauffer that was replaced with a non-Black babysitter. The Black orderly in the hospital morgue, however, remained consistent in both earlier and later script adaptations.

Conceptually, the opening credits with a black background and white script tell us from the outset (as the narration of Black slaves did in the first script) that aspects of our seeing will be held in stark relief, including race as black, negative space. I don't think this was a coincidence. For example in the mirroring of the two parties, Ziegler's holiday party had a smattering of Black extras elegantly dressed and dancing. In the ballroom of the Long Island mansion, where nude and clothed masked people are dancing, there is no Black presence. This is a "Whites Only" club. I feel that Kubrick is deliberately making a point of this. It's a racial, political point about the nature of power in upper echelons. (I was even more firmly convinced of this point when I read that Gayle, the model whom Bill Harford had given his handkerchief to, was a Black woman in an earlier script.)

Bill thought he was at the top, that he knew about life but he was the ingénue who needed saving. His wife, much more sophisticated in the way sexuality works, was forthright in disabusing Bill of his smug, naïve notions. It's what women have to learn in order to survive, to "play" the virgin, the inaccessible woman, to move up in the world. The way she handled the macking by Sandor Savzost vs. the way Bill was overwhelmed by the models ("Where are we going, exactly?") demonstrates Alice's smarts and mobility are much more formidable than Bill's. Her frustration with him, after they start getting high, was triggered by the revelation of his smugness. She decided to "wipe the smug look off his face" by telling him a tale, trying to hip him to get out of his mental bubble. That story about her temptation by the officer shakes Bill up, preparing him psychologically, for the turn of events ahead of him that night.

Of course the film *Eyes Wide Shut*, which features a secret group of powerful people who "punish" those who reveal their inner workings, along with Kubrick's untimely demise soon after completion, leads to inevitable conspiracy theories. In looking at a few of the archives on the film, including Kubrick's research materials, the only noteworthy thing I found was that Kubrick looked up technical aspects of what that secret group might feasibly look like, to create the scene, just as he looked up Venetian masks and other aspects of Middle Ages Italian Renaissance culture. (In the original script, the naked women in masks and the men in robes were dressed up as priests and nuns.)

The shady dealings that I think Kubrick may have been alluding to, and that I think I read someplace in the volumes of webpages I've come across over the years, is that Alice may have been part of the entire operation (which is why we saw her nude and dropping a black gown at the very beginning). That, as Ziegler said, was a "set up" but the set up was to break Bill down. My theory is that this is the way they introduce people into the group. Everyone is in on it and no one's talking. (Yes, I do think Amanda was murdered, and Kubrick wanted to insinuate that she was.) There was one gesture that was the "tell" for me: when Ziegler is telling everything to Bill, at the end, he puts his hands on Bill's shoulders from behind, in a way that makes Bill cringe. In one of the scripts, (it may have been Raphael's 1997 version. By the way, I've incorporated just a few words that were in other script versions, for fun, into the poem.) it says something to the affect that Ziegler puts his hands on Bill's shoulders, "reassuringly." I don't know what Pollack may have had in mind when he performed the gesture but Kubrick kept it, knowing, by Cruise's reaction, that it didn't come across as reassuring and may not have intended to be so. So what was its affect? Intimidation, fear. Ziegler also seemed to know way more about Amanda Curran's death than his flippant tone would imply, certainly more than was in the papers. (If one freeze-frames the still of the newspaper, one can read the text. This was before DVDs could freeze-frame with clarity so the text is superfluous and even repetitious and non-grammatical. However, the brevity of the article also indicates that Ziegler knew lots more, and had memorized more, about her death than a general reader would and was well-versed in the alibi that the murderers would use after she was killed.)

The beauty of the women and the beauty of the lead man were frequently burdens. In Harford/Cruise's case, his male beauty brought him attention and aggression from men and women. It was not a shield but an opening. His naiveté, far from being empowering as innocence, betrayed him at every turn. The "tree of knowledge" was necessary to survive.

And speaking of iconic stories…Alice's provocation of other men is a domain she easily manipulates. Her intelligence in the face of a naïve man invokes Amiri Baraka's play, *Dutchman,* in which innocent Clay is also deliberately sent to his doom by a woman, Lula, who knew all the moves beforehand. (Alice is specifically connected to Eve in earlier versions of the script.) In both stories, someone died. Clay thought his masculinity, would protect him but there were larger forces at work than he realized. When Bill Harford says "Gentlemen" after the man in the purple robe says "Remove your clothes" Harford is appealing to other men to protect him. They don't. He's not on their level. He's punished for being an interloper, presuming that he belongs because of the qualities he was born with and ones that he has earned through hard work. The Zieglers of the world don't have to work, but they play very hard indeed (the only activities we see Ziegler engaged in, and that he describes, are recreational: drugs, sex, drinking, billiards and tennis). And this is why Bill Harford cannot just "slip in." Everyone else at the party knows who's behind all the other masks. Alice would never have presumed she could just slip unknown into the party. (I do, however, think she was there.)

I guess, after all this time, I finally understand why this film has been a favorite of mine for over a decade, why it kept nagging at me. It's a film about power of a specific kind, the type that is bound up in the identity of those who truly wield it, the ones who are unseen. I don't mean that in a paranoid way, I mean it in the way that one can readily recognize Tom Cruise's face and the privilege he typifies, as well as Nicole Kidman's, but not the captains of corporations and their billionaire scion which really run things that manifest in our everyday lives. This isn't because of secret meetings in a sex club, it's because of the power they amass through connections. In *Eyes Wide Shut* it's super secret sexual connections but it alludes to something more banal and real than occasional mystical sexual play.

I think Kubrick deliberately made a film about this topic, about power, our fantasies, about how we think we control our lives and how other people do through their positions, insularity and mutual support. Kubrick grew up as a Jewish New Yorker from the Bronx, haunted by his family's intimate knowledge of the Holocaust. His father Jacob was a "prominent" doctor and could have connected to people above his class. It's possible that Kubrick was intrigued by the mystery of that class, its allure vs. reality.

Schnitzler's text would be an excellent way to explore all these issues, the desire for fantasy and the coldness of reality: "As so often in Schnitzler, death functions as an intensifying factor in the sexual adventure… The actuality of death destroys the magic of heightened sensuality… The pleasure garden has changed into the desire. The skeleton is now seen forcing its way through the once alluring flesh." This quote is from an article that Kubrick used for his research (*Arthur Schnitzler: A Critical Study.* Chapter V 'Morals and Psyscho-analysis', New Clarion Press, 1971) this particular series of sentences were underlined by Kubrick himself.

Codas

Alice's last word:

The last word in the screenplay is coarse: "Fuck." It wasn't in earlier versions of the script. (I've sprinkled a few words and ideas, here and there, of earlier Kubrick/Raphael script drafts in the poem). And Alice says "you know what we have to do as soon as possible." This is Alice removing the romance of their marriage as she did when Bill wanted to use the word "Forever" earlier in this scene. Alice wants the bare truth, the knowing truth, to be told and to be expressed. You can see the hint of the adage "the truth shall set us [sexually, knowingly] free" in the comedy "Mr. & Mrs. Smith" featuring another Hollywood "it" couple, Angelina Jolie and Brad Pitt (who, unlike Cruise and Kidman, married after the making of this film, which was a jumping off point for their relationship, according to press accounts). That honest sex is better than dishonest sex and that knowledge is power, it's charged. This is the only way of getting past the challenges of the last two days by giving oneself over to the other honestly, without masks.

The last note I want to make is about my style of writing this handholding exercise with Kubrick. I found it a bit of a challenge to "converse" in this way, but it was enjoyable. In my sound work I often employ repetition and here I found simple repetition and rhyme to work most efficiently in this "collaboration." There is a very strong rhythmic energy in Kubrick's filmmaking and this film in particular. Adjusting to that energy was visceral and fun but certainly different from my own. As we get "deeper down the rabbit hole" of the "dream story" I found the rhythm and rhyme required needed to be more overt. By the time I got to the credits I also wanted to add a bit of levity as the music was infectious. It's the only overt humor, that's not dark humor, in this entire section.

Ultimately I find *Eyes Wide Shut* to be a strange film, a disturbing film, a subtle horror story, a wonderful enjoyable masterpiece as many of Kubrick's films are. In my playing with this film, I want to create a (possibly) alternative narrative in which Bill is being prepped to join this group by manipulating him, breaking his mind and then drawing him in (and ensuring that he keeps the group's secrets). Of course I'm not arguing that this is what Kubrick intended, I'm certainly not arguing that's what Arthur Schnitzler intended. I was interested in extending the idea they both constructed beyond the dream state and into a possible future, a new, permanent reality for Bill. I guess this was my way of showing gratitude to Kubrick, by extending the speculation of his story beyond his life, especially since he didn't have the chance to clarify his intent as he passed away soon after the film's completion.

Here's to Kubrick's genius and thanks to you for reading and listening to this play with one of the works of the master players.

The audio for "*eyes wide shut:* a not neo-benshi read" is available at korepress.org/TracieMorris

eyes wide shut: a not-neo benshi read

Wardens, close in, capture. Brothers put things where they belong.

The scariest people in the world are not Black
The scariest people in the world are not Black
The scariest people in the world are not Black
The scariest people in the world are not Black
The scariest people in the world are not Black

She slips on Black sometimes, then slips it off.

In high relief, Black is the background
In high relief, Black is the background

White is at the forefront, couple letters, couple notes
White is at the forefront, couple letters, couple notes
White is at the forefront, couple letters, couple notes

Honey, get it together lets go: where's the money?

"Isn't it on the bedside table?"

"Now lissen." Glissen lissen glissen lissen. "I know"

I don't wash my hands first. Let's be a little dirty
I don't wash my hands first. Let's be a little dirty.

You look like a swan Leda, your hands aren't clean.
Afterthought splashing: Zeus detritus, Odin's seed.

(Dry on blue. The driest blue.) "All right, all right"
I'm ready.

A small man with money gets a tall woman
A small man with money gets a tall woman

He stacks up and she lies down

What's the name of the baby sitter baby? Where's the baby?
What's the name of the baby sitter baby? Who's the baby?

We're rich enough to have a White one
Rich enough to have a White one.
Enough to have a White one.

You even know her "The Nutcracker"
Know her, name her. No 'er name 'er noer
namer noer namer noer namer noer namer
A little late for that.

Wriggling fingers, a hand signal, a little girl. I see ya.

Walk down the runway. We're the winners.
Walk down the runway, we're the winners.

Star celebrate: the holidays.
What kind of star? What day is today?

Victor, victor. Trophy, trophy. Victor, victor trophy trophy.
Yes he does. Red wearing wife knows what he loves.

I make a fist, I touch you.

("I touch you")

We're close but not that close. Close but not that close.
Closer, clothes. Closer clothes. The closers. White star trellis, electric flowers.
White star trellis, electric flowers.

Harnessing the white their: contained and pretty.

White ceilings and floors, lights and people.
White ceilings and floors,
Lights and people.

"Not a soul."

"This is what you get"… this is what you get, is what you get.

Could it be more obvious than white keys? More obvious white keys?
Overt white keys. Overwhite, a key.

Rich enough to have a white *band*. Band in white. "You see that guy?"

"Thank you." … Bandy about white.

White couple splits. She says to W.C. W.C. W.C
We'll see, we'll see.

Sipping more comfortable. Cover comfort, slipping.

Singer in the coal mine, Nightingale canary.
Sounder in the coalmine, nightingale canary.
"Oh my God, Bill. How long's it been?"

No yellow feathers he's plucked over.
White feathers, white feathers, white feathers.
Pointed, features.

I'm touching. You're touching me.
I'm touching you. You're touching me.

"Not too bad." 'sup doc. You a pianist.
"Well, my friends call me that."

"I never did understand."
A lot less than you think.

No fraternizing artist, you're the help.
Nightingale. Help. The help. Canary.
Help, help. Canary. Seeing you,
seeing you the help. Seeing you seeing you help.

Touch me touching you touch me, man. My God. Surprise.
Two Black bow ties, black exes, over whites of his eyes.

…

Turns from one to too. You. Thirsty. I want some. I want some.
Nice glass. My glass. "I'm absolutely certain." I swallow, birdie. Thirst
My name is a snake, snack, snake – a snake. Good eve.

Tall man wants a small woman, can see down her front.
Tall man wants a small woman, can see down her front.
Apple breasts, lovely. Forgive me, if I'm blunt.

Eyes out. *Eyes* out.

Let's talk costs baby. How much do you know?
Let's talk value honey, how much do you know?
White noise, classy lady. Go baby go. Go baby, go!

Takes her for a test drive, a test drive, test. Testing.
"What do you do?" Let's get to the money. The money, the money.

I can get you some. I can get you,
get you, get you. Sums. Sums.

Flowers under a tree with dark bark: Petals 'round the décolletage.
You know you know you know you know. I know you know…

How rings around the rosies go. Rings around the rosies go.
Oooh Oh!
Oooh oh uh oh. Oooh oh uh oh. Oooh oh uh oh:

(Alice is the rabbit hole.)

Money & marriage: m&m make the deal.
Make the deal, make the deal. Make the deal — as good as that.

…

Me & you and her are cute. Me & you and her are cute.
Me & you and her on cue. On cue. A spelled name, a spell.

Let's broach the subject of your sex. Segue to sex. Snake.
Broaching her draped on his lapel.

Work the knowledge
work the knowledge.

Too hard? Harder, harder
I bet, I know.

Exactly. Exactly.

Let's find out. What you know, doc.
(A lot less than you think.)

…

The top of the staircase has a dead chick.
The top of the staircase has a dead chick.

And a man with suspenders putting in his dick.
And a man in suspenders putting in his dick.

Chick behind him and a chick in front.
Chick behind him and a chick in front.

You know what I can rhyme here.
(You know I won't.)

Move your head, Mandy.
Can you move your head? That's right.

Open your eyes.
Open your eyes. You're *ice*.

Look at me, Mandy. I'm a man. Mandy. I'm a man.
Look when I say, dammit. I'm a man. Good. Good.

…

Baby let's make it quick. Let's go up.
Chill around the statues, cold as f--k.

…

The bathroom again, big as my house.
Blue, feral drying mess. Dead water mouse.

You know that. You know that.
I know. I know. You.

Victor the victor, wants to take out the trash.
Wins, wants to take out trash.
Can't ruin the party for a little snatch.
Helluva party in a little snatch.

Snatch her snatch snack.
Snatch her snatch back.

Two men talk about man things.
Two men talk about man things.
Both of them know how the dick swings.
Both of them know which way the dick swings.
…

Star bright life of the party, lampshade halo

I think I have to go now. Go baby go! Go baby go!

Of course you will…

Yes. I do. No I won't.

Drunk but not that drunk. Feelin' lucky punk?
Keeps his hands on, jerky with his spunk.

…

Look in the looking glass. Nods to herself.
Looks in the mirror nods to herself.
Sees another world, puts glasses on the shelf.
Open eyes on a shelf.

Look into the mirror sneaking tongues.
Speaking tongues. They're speaking tongues.
"Alright. I'm ready."

…

Steel accordion elevator smug man comes out
Steel accordion elevator smug man comes out

Bright day ahead. Is there ever any doubt?
Smiles and orders. Never done, without.

Nice being a housewife, house like that
Spices in the background, cartoon living with a rugrat

…

Chin up son, you'll be just like me
Chin up. We're wanted. Watch tv?

…

Not a drop of fat on her 'cept in the right places
Long legs like that she's ready for the races
Philly like that, goes through the paces.

…

Another leg up,
Another White male says yeah.
Doc's takes care of him, he's taking care.

…

Both getting ready, pheromones are important
Both getting ready, pheromones are important
Van Gogh in perfect present, wrapping's not distorted
Lovingly contorted.

Girl starting early, takes years to get ready
Start early kid, takes years to get ready.
Just like momma by the time you're going steady
Prep to get the guy. It gets *heady*.

…

Sticking to the niceties is how you keep your business
Sticking to the niceties is how you keep your business
It's "what you get."

How do you feel? How do you feel?
About wrapping? Rapping? Telling.

I look. I look. I see what's here, what's coming.
Band-aid. Let's fix this thing. Fix is in. Fixin' in.

…

Tell me some thing. some thing. (deep weeds)
Those two: thing one, thing two.

Did you did you? Happen to?
What are you?

I'm talking. I'm talking.

I wasn't hitting. I wasn't on.

Oh.

the models. new models?
the (old one) models.

that man. what did he want?
what did he want? what did he want.

then and there?

that was. that was. That's all.
That's right.

Whoa. Whoa. What you're saying?
What men *are* alike?

There are exceptions. what makes you
What makes me. What makes you

I happen to be. I happen to be.
Exceptional. *married*.

(*Well you know why people get married*, said the snake to Eve.
Snakeven. Shaken. Victor's married.)

I'm not arguing. I'm just trying to find out.
Let's find out.

Sex is the last thing.
The last thing on.

She's afraid. Afraid of what I might…

Women don't… think
like that. Women don't… think
(like that?)

***Right! Right?

Alice says to Cheshire. You are very very sure.
You are very very sure.
You are very very sure sure of sure of you.

If you only knew.

Funny. Fucking … fit.
Funny. Fucking

Fit fit fit.

Alice turns him out.
Turn about, turned out, he's tuned out.

[don't be so sure, bill.]

bell, bill. bell, bill. bell, bill.

Ding!

He was checking in.

Ding!

The elevator.

Ding!

You have his attention Alice.

If he wanted me… I was ready. "I'm ready."
Ready for me. Ready me. Steady glance,
Steadicam.

My fucking future.
weird, weird, weird, dear.

tender. mercy.
Attender. Tend tend tend her.

sad. mercy.

slept. My love for you slept.

Even if it was only for one night
Even if it was only for one night
Even if it was only for one night

My love. My love.
My love. My love.

I barely. Bare.

Might still be there.
He might still.

I was. IwasIwasIwas. I-I-I

Relieved.

[sighs.]

[timely: phone rings. a ding-a-ling]

When did it happen.
When did it happen.

Thank you.
Thank you.

Just died. Show my face.

Car car car beep
Beep peep.

Peep show peep show peep show
Panties.

Violin strings, strings, strings. Heart.

Ding dong.

Ding!

Black and white and Latina maid
Rose. Answers.

In the bedroom. Not so good.
Knock knock

A little tree.

Marion. Maid.

Dumbstruck.

I'm a bit numb. Numb, numb.
Sunk in. sunk pump. Punk.

Body number one. Father.
Unbothered. Unreal.

Good day, good day, Daddy.
"You do not do, you do not do
Any more, black shoe" *

Peacefully in his sleep.
Sleep, sleep, sleep.

Death itself.

He'll be over. Carl's cold calling.
He's over.

Math in May. Professor not teacher.

Michigan. Miss again.
You're in a beautiful state.

Did her eyes roll back?
Roll Michigan, shaking a river. Dive in.
Dowsing rod tongue. Losing water, tears.

I um, I love you. I yum.
I um. I um I um um.
I hum.

I don't want. I want.
Even if, even if, even if.

---

* From "Daddy" by Sylvia Plath, from *The Collected Poems by Sylvia Plath*,
published by Harper & Row. Copyright © 1981

For one night. My whole future.

We barely know
Even if even if even if

[timely: bell ringing]

You despise.

Down a runway, not a winner.
Down a runway, not a winner.

What kind of kiss was that? A Carl kiss.
Kind of cooling.

Okay.

I touch you. I touch you.

He wipes off lipstick. Slick, clean handkerchief.
Looking finger, finger-licking. Thinking finger.
Slips cross, crooks.

Three men, one dead, and a woman.
Three men, one dead, and a woman.
Only one's not tense. (He's past it.)

These last months. Mum.
Months. Mum months.

Did you see her soul leave?
…

Breath of fresh, getting it together.
Fresh air, composure, exposure fresh.

I touch me. I hit. I touch me.

More desire sir and sire, sire sire.
Violins and shimmer. Restaurants

Boys offer an in—an invite.
Boys offer an in—an invite.

He's mad at the Mrs. Boys offer an in, sight:

What is it about – him?
Bout me? What is it about, round about me?

Wanna piece of this, prime cut?
Everyone tags him, he's the butt.

He's not ready for these streets, these streets, these streets.
Man alive, man you. What kinda you?

…

Have a little? Have a little? Have a little?

Come inside with you. Nicer in there.
In their, in there there.

No one will bother. It's okay.
A bigger tree. Brighter than Marion.

Do you suppose we should? Guess.

What do want to do?
What do you do? Wanna?

[hearty laugh. Heart to laugh]

I'd rather not put it.
Put it.

I'm in your…

…

"If I was Italian you would've answered me in Italian."

Light, another kiss, permission.
Piano player tickling ivory, playing keys.

Presence of mind a turn off. His first time?

Timely call: Much longer?

Why is she waiting?
Why isn't she dreaming?
…

Happy pair on tv tiring me.
Now, not now, now.

…

Mrs. Dr. What are you doing?
Doctor's wife,

Do I have to go. [Thought you'd never ask.]

You don't have to.
I want to. Thank you.

…

Sweet dreams, a sonata.
Wide awake, café. Blue colors, notes.
4 men, quartet. 4 men, 4 hours, horses.

A brother opens doors. Clear-headed.

Looks over his shoulder.

…

A table – cough – la mesa
Cat's got SK's tongue

Can I take you?
Can I take you? (Somewhere over…)

1,2, 1,2,3,4

Nick Night
Nick Night

Good. Great.
Great, Thanks.

Your last set.

Blink blink, nightingale
Blink blink. Canary.

You made it.

1,2, 1,2,3,4 boys
1 wife.

You gotta go. You gotta go. Work.

Thank you. (Doesn't the band get free drinks?)
Who pays?

A pickup. Anybody, anywhere. A pianist.
My friends call me.

Another night.

Another night.

I don't actually know.

So far. So far.
A different place.

Mystery. I just play.
Men talk. I just play.
(Wriggling fingers. I see you.)
Childhood monster.
I just play.

Excuse.

Nick I'm sorry.
Never a doctor, never a doctor.
Nick I'm sorry. Sorry canary.

Playing blind. Flying blind.
I play.

What? What what?
You're putting me.

Man. I have seen, blind.
One or two things, blind
I have one or two things.

Never anything.
Never such
Never such
Women. Such women.
Never never never. [Lenore]
mmmm.

[timing: a phonecall]

Brrrrring!
Bring bring bring.
Mmhm: Fidelio Deelio.
On my way, says the nightingale

The password.
The pass.

Listen. One second.
Gotta go. Gotta gotta go.
Into the coal. Into the cold.

A break, break break.
Gimme a beak, gimme.
Singing sweetly, first.

Mischievous. Let's just say.
Let's just say. I told you.

Everyone is masked.
The hell. A costume.
A custom. Costume. A trial balloon.

…

Rainbow, rainbow.
Follow the yellow cab.
Where the rainbow ends.
Hey Dorothy?
(missing hearts, brains, nerve, en toto)

Bill ingénue, looking to play dress.
Article of clothing, just not ruby red:

You abuzz? Yes.

The owner.
The doctor.

Grenning went to greener pastures.
Grenning, greener. The hawk came for him.

Yes. I am. Once a doctor. Always.
Proud. I own.

Millich. Froggy. Cold-blooded creature.

Okay. So you are doctor.

Please please, please.
Don't go oh oh oh.
I need.

I'd pay over. Rainbow over the price.

I don't think so.
(I see you. Pot of gold. You see me.)

More over?

…

Yes. Okay. Beep beep.
Alarm – cough – alarm.

Come in (side with me).
Can't be careful.
mmmm.

Is it any special… you're looking?

Yes.

I think we find something
for you. [Purrrrs.]

Follow me.

Looks like alive, huh?
Huh? Huh?

White curtain trellis, electric flowers.
Dancing still life.

Black. Black black.
(The scariest people in the world wear black.)

Are you sure?

Black. Hood. Mask.
Shadows.

You are medicine?

I'm afraid.

I'm in hurry too doctor.
Get to bed. Sssh.

[thump]

…

What is it?
(not the first time she's slipped)

Bless you.

The body reveals,
The body tells on you. An invitation.

Girl dresses up, dresses down.

Two men invited by a small woman.
A small woman in small clothes.

Chopsticks upright in foam.
Sign of death.

Millich quotes Joseph Welch.
Your conscience telling on yourself?

But the girl, the girl.
"If you men only knew…"

Gentlemen.
Please. Police.

My customer. Sorry.
Please! I'm trying to serve!
These Gentlemen!

Men have business to do.
This chick is part of business.

Baby girl, plays dress up.
Plays doctor, play.

She she she secret.
She Leelee's secret.
Sobieski secret. Snake. Good Eve.

Seaman sees more and more.
Seaman sees more.

Doctor recollects why
He cracked this door.

Suburb see more.
Submerge some more.

Somerton.
They summer.

He repeats money, says again.
Money honey. Waiting for me. Wait.

I'll leave my stuff.
We'll run you up.

Red car red run red car red run red car red run

...

Baroque ornate baroque ornate
Locate a special date

Ballet gesture with a golden masque
Ballet gesture with a golden masque

You asked to enter.
You asked, asked.

Masque of red death did you read the story
Masque of red death did you read the story

Slicker than rich linen an elegant gory
Slicker than rich linen inelegant glory

Kettle drums kettle drums what is that piping
Kettle drums kettle drums what is that piping

People in Venetian masks with their distended smiling
People in Venetian masks with their distended smiling

Nick night Nick Night in a black tie
Nick night Nick Night in a black tie

Matching blindfold makes the organs sigh
Matching blindfold makes the organs sigh.

Bill Harford has a butterfly face
Tornado in the making past this day.

Caterpillaring the street, bowing in this temple place
Caterpillar it's dreaming 'til wings give him grace

Perky breasts and g strings never know their face
Perky breasts and g strings, waiting in this space.

Look at the array of things watching all the beauty
Whispering creatures. Assessing treasures, booty.

Gamine gamines are game.
Gamine gamines are game.
Strutting intention. No one's to blame.

A robotic turn like Hal, no face
Discerns how you enter, your grace.

That tear in prison known as a tell
Country Dr. doesn't know it as well.
Doesn't know it well.

Everyone knows who's who at this ball.
That look is what you get – for making house calls.

Biggest headdress chooses best.
Biggest headdress chooses best.

Biggest plumes have the nicest nest.
Is she breathing, nodding yes?

…

Even with a mask on, that lovely knows he's fine.
Even with a mask on, that lovely knows he's fine.
Kiss to kiss porcelain, nectar of divine.

Look at her clavicle look at her, awes
Look at her clavicle locked at the jaws

Gliding down the aisle gelding on hind paws
Gliding with the G, he's clueless of the laws.

I have to let your hand go but you have to keep it steady.
Keep it steady keep it steady keep it steady.
In the beginning, redhead says it's heady.

I know that voice of yours. Hearing you confirms it.
"Look at me" you once said. here's a head's up, you deserve it.

I may not know my way around but why you let him take your girl?
I may not know my way around but why you let him take your girl?
The way you let her hand go, is the way this night unfurls.

The night unfurls.

…

We're at the half-point, after midnight. Switching hour worlds.
Worlds turning worlds turning, switching our worlds.

Some folks watch and some folks do.
Some folks watch and some folks do.

Some folks latch on, others drawn in, drew.

Baroque wallpaper glistening with dew.

Bill watching, walking through, with his game face on.
Bill watching, walking through, with his gameface on.
Intrigued to say the least, tries to cool his internal storm.

His internal storms. Nothing that he's acting on.

…
Naked woman told to saunter wants to keep him warm.
Flyest feathered lady, pulls him from the swarm.

(Who's the woman who has a dress on? Dress on? Dress on?)

…

Strangers in the night is playing, dropping one last hint.
Look at me, reversing order, time to flee little prince.

…

Dude in so out of his depth, can't see the axehead glints.
Mask he wears everyday is his doe-eyes squint.

Doe-eyes squint. Sharpness of the flint.
'bout to flinch man, you're about to flinch.

…

Someone's at the door sure as hell ain't your driver.
Someone's at the door, surely ain't your driver.

You're in the zone man.
You ain't no high flyer, baby. You ain't no high flyer.

Canary is the Nightingale taken to the coal mine.
All the glitz around him, and he's become the gold-dined.

Canary out of gilded cage, end of his music stint.
Featherless, skint.

...

Glad you're wearing robes man, you're about to graduate.
Woman tried to help you out, now it's just too late.

...

Scariest are open mouths with no sound coming out.
Wariest open mouthed people, no sound coming out.
They're Munch originals, know what they're about.

When he said please come forward, that was the cue to run away
You heard him say come forward and you didn't run away?
You're like the chicks in horror flicks who back into the fray.

Password password have you any fools?
Yes sir yes sir pigeon pigeon stools.

(He knows a lot less than you think.)

May I ask may I ask, may I ask may I ask?
What's the task what's the task what's the task?

Kindly remove masking.
Blindly leaning shaking not asking

Social circle social life, drowning Technicolor bath
Technicolor bath, basking basking,

In the house, house, house.
There's a mouse, mouse, mouse.

Remove your clothes. We loathe, we loathe.

Bend then break him. Naked then take him.

…

Take *me* take me. Let him go.
Ring around the (woe woe woe)

redeem redeem
Munch screams, murmur dreams

free warning free warning.
Warned warmed go.
Discreet, giving chickadee—no no no!

Look at her look at her body of life.
Birdie in a tree with a mask, looks like a scythe.
Death itself, a scythe, sight, scythe, sight, scythe.

Promises, promises, damask, sorrow.
Lucky you once again. Go she said: Go!

…

In the home in the home.
Safer place, now he knows

Baby cakes and pretty cheeks
Radiate from street light below.
Below below below. Daddy is so sallow.

What a night, after day. Displace masks
Wishing all away.

…

Alice laughing again. Why is she so glad?
"Thought you were having a nightmare." Laughing?

Wants to give her "something to laugh at."

Horrible. Horrible. Dream. Took longer.
Weird things. Ready for something stronger?

You still want her to tell you what she imagines?
You know what's coming. Why are you asking?

…

Imagine a deserted city with Martha and George.
Naked – "Remove your clothes."

As Adam and Eve. Ashamed. You, ran away.
I felt wonderful. Then I was lying, I could finally play.

In a Garden. Naked. In a garden. A man walks out
The navel. The naked navel. He glanced about.

"But that's not the end" he says. Yes sir yes sir. 3 more clues.
He knew he knew he knew before she told the "truth."

"Why don't you tell me the rest?"
Arrest? A dream.

He's seen the scene play out already.
What can be worse than real life?

People around us. Everyone was.
Then I was. I lost. Lost count.

I knew you could see. I knew you could.
I wanted to make … fun. To laugh. So I did.
"If you men only knew."

All those people around. She knows what's up.

All the way down. (was in one of the masks and gowns)

The looking glass of Alice's dreams. Her accurate fantasies, alarming.
Going on a fishing trip when you're the one she's farming.

…

William Harford's checking in. First at the Sonata.
Bill's keeping doctors' hours. Not everyone oughta.

Know Nick, know Nick?

…

She's tasting sweets behind the coffee cup
Almost licking, biting, lips. Waitress waiting up.

Why'd she give him Nick's info.? A friend would already know it.
Just who is who to whom here? Bill's down the road she's shown him.

Alan Cumming hubba hubba-ing. Gives him all the details.
Looking at Cruise like sliced meat, dipping paws in entrails, entrails,
entrails.

A little on the … side. A little on the … side.
Grin is wide, grin is wide wide wide.

Can you tell on the canary? Sing, can you sing?
Bill the birdie, beak and feathers ruffling.

He's leaning in to lay it thick, Bill is closer.
'bout to tell a whopper, lead Bill where he's supposed 'ta.

Big eyes. (wide open)

Not the kind of men you wanna fool around with,

If you know what I mean (Hey Dorothy)

Bill's back on the yellow road to give Milich his stuff.
He doesn't tell Milich everything, how the night was a bit rough.

Milich looks better in the day, is that a velvet vest?
Contrasting tie and buttons, looks a bit overdressed.

Sorry for the mask, sorry, with a side grin.
You're a moneyed doc, right? Take it on the chin.
For the mask…wonder what place it's in.

Gentle men walk out with good manners
Two men you may know.
Grey haired and pauses, he's seen Bill.
One blows a kiss as kudos. Kudos girl, kudos

He's got queries, he's got shock. He's got queries, he's got shock.
Missy has been over the moon, around the block.

He was going to call the cops, but joined chickadee on the stroll.
Don't be so naïve Bill, you bought some several hours ago.

…

Doctor is distracted and cannot see his patients.
Getting on the road to learn the steep gradient.

Isn't Dr. Harford cute. First a cab and now a jeep.
Driving to the edge of the island where the learning curve is steep.
He's stewing in his thinking. Let him steep.

Doctor's brash with a moral chip, got to admire his moxie.
Head up he looks direct, in camera, through it to its proxy.

They saw him coming from miles away.
Brought the car round *sin* delay.

Nice paper nice paper always sends a message.
Dicey baby, dicey baby. Second chance is sufficient.

Give up on idealism, man. That lady gave permission.
They knew your name and title, This group isn't kiddin'.
They really aren't kidding.

Daddy's home daddy's home pretending all is well.
Kiss the mother, pet the girl in the traumnouvelle. Swell daddy swell.

Helena is learning. Play it smart and get ahead.
Helena is learning. Play it smart and get ahead.
Good answers get good marriage, instead – of what?—instead.

Helena wants a puppy—and really can you blame her?
All about her is this stuff, a big dog to play will train her.
Tame her tame her train her.

What's Joe got, what's Joe got? More than Mike by a lot.
Figure out what Joe's got honey.

He looks at her with a glare. She looks back and smiles.
The distances between the two go for country miles.
An estate on a country mile. …

Camera pans a scene with one small white door that's ajar.
Close up to the doctor's eyes. He's looking at afar.

Dr. tries to be a baller. Realizes that it's not him.
Bad timing as he's calling. His nerves begin to thin.

The lotto store the lotto store.
Take your chances with a red-door.

(Another person who's not in. The 3rd since his
rewind begins: Nick, Dom, Marian)

Sally forth, not Domino but she's got some sugar for ya.
What's in the bakery box that's tastier than her flora?

Come in Bill come in. Domino said you were nice bill.
Had a nice build, hands nice bills.

He looks excited and a little nervous.
Her looks slice, as the hotel clerk's did.

Repeating Domino's location that is to say she isn't there.
Clarify Domino's insinuation, Sally says she isn't here.
Bill's feeling optimistic and forward. Bringing Christmas cheer.

"So when the woman is having her 'titties' squeezed by handsome Dr. Bill,
Do you think she might be wondering what his dickie might be like?
Hmm?"

Not taking off your tie,
Pulling your coat to the side.

"You don't quite know how." "I bet you're knowledgeable about
all sorts of things" but now you don't know how.

That face of his in that space.
Hail hookers full of grace.

Tells Bill the truth about Domino, game of chance he won at the end.
He's one at the end. At the other end. No joke status, no pretend.

He was tapping his finger and he stopped when he heard her.
Happily tapping finger, stopped when he heard her.
Lucky he didn't tap that, Bill's more of a flirter. (Dr. wouldn't hurt her.)

Bill can't catch a lucky break. Thought he was gonna get some.
Traversing the streets, he marks a flake. Camel reed coat by his lonesome.

White star trellis, electric, flowers, in another scene.
"This isn't a dream."

Two gentlemen by Verona, with a hint of lace.
There's masks and their removal, undergarments under place.

Never took his eyes off, Harford's lucky to be alive.
Ducks into a speakeasy will gasp at what's inside.

Extras in deep conversation,
In the paper, what's inside.
Bill shaken, in today's ruminations
Another scary ride. The end that she decides.

…

He has to see for sure, has the ins and outs to know.
He has to follow up, house calling a case to close.

A spelled name, a spilled name, a spell.

…

He has to see her for himself.
He has her pulled out from under the shelf.

The orderly keeps order here.
Pays respects and disappears.

The least scary people in the film are not White:
He, Rosa, a doorman at night.
Wear 3 kinds of uniforms: Orderly black, blue and white, black
and blue and white.

…

Doctor making a house call, "this is what you get"

Call timing is prescient, checkerboard set.

Checkered, greying 2nd corpse within 24 hours.
Repressed Bill somewhat upset. Death made the doctor dour.

…

I touch you. Victor knocking balls around. Halls around, balls around.
A 25 year old. Gird your loins, Bill. He's up for another round.

Talk about something awkward? Bill's grin stifling laughter
I saw you with an O.D.'ed hooker, zipping up your pants after.
Now shy manly banter?

Bill's trying to hold it together. Pretend his life's the same.
Ziegler knows the extent of it, just short of naming names.
He's not going to name names.

Nick whatever the fuck though
shouldn't have put you in the frame.

You know who… you know who.
I had no idea… I had no idea… I had no, idea.

I know you didn't Bill. I had you followed, not alone.
I'm throwing you a bone, Bill, take it, go home.

Nick was bruised for what he said, isn't a hell of a lot.
There's a lady in the morgue, Nick's only got a clot.

You know who… Remains nameless.

Woman tried to warn me. Tried to warm me.
I know, no-no.

Just a hooker, Bill. A looker. Hooked up Bill, look look.
A no-name. Woman unknown.

Suppose Bill, suppose. Let's imagine. Let's play.
All of that world's a stage. A charade. Then what's fake?

Bill claps at the successful show.
But wheels are turning. What doesn't go?

Bill knows something with his doctor's mind.
Victor's surely lying, Bill saw her death note's sign.

Way out of depth. Deep end of pool table:
They took her home. She was fucked but fine.
Victor knows more than the paper said. Is he being kind?

How's he know how the door was locked?
Did she open it when he knocked?

Victor had to say so, or Bill would have to report him
Being a doctor, revealing all things mortem

Grip of death on Bill's shoulders.
Harford shivers, blood runs colder.

I put my death grip on your shoulders only 'cause we're friends.
Flinching shoulders bunchin up Bill. Let's talk present tense.

…

Look at all the gifts under the tree, you don't want to lose them.
Christmas is coming, look at the tree, you don't want to lose them.
Wise men gave gifts to the baby, twinkle twinkle amusement.

Looks like a menorah there but red candles and two short.
Almost a menorah on the right, red candles but two short.
Holidays don't quite measure up, a missing aspect of some sort.

Christmas is around the corner. Enough surprises for a day.
Beer to steady his nerves. Everything's okay. At home everything's okay.

...

He paid for that mask already and now he's paying again.
He paid for that mask already and now he's paying again.
Wanted to put it all behind him but not able to pretend. Story never ends.
Alice never looks at the mask. Who put it there? Did she have it last?
Why does she look at him and not the gold that's glinting?
Alice holds him tenderly, sad. Not a hint of flinching.

Bill is lowering to her holds his heart where he loosened his tie.
Beating stops, then slowly starts, this man's about to cry.
Cry cry cry cry. Stoic man's wailing his cries.

He breaks down and she's not wincing.
Very very sure… so convincing.

Masks are missing from the bed, from Bill.
She's finishing her tasks. Warming him up for the next bash.

(Do you know why Ziegler invites you to these things?)

Another camel reed coat, a slow, deliberate gait.
Keeping up appearances, Helena's future's at stake.

Camel reed coat, black sweater.
Keeping it together's the kicker.
A smooth slim sister, straight out
Of a noir flick. Flick, flick flicker.

Helena Helena wants her gift
Helena Helena senses the rift

Helena Helena wants her toy
Helena Helena play horse Troy.

The next line of lovely for a lovely boy.
Making a new Alice, a red beauty, coy.

Something's still fishy. Koi, koi, koi.

Real pretty, it's old-fashioned.
Real pretty, it's old-fashioned.
Tradition plays a big part here. Change is strictly rationed.

[Helena gives a knowing glance.
She's growing up quickly too.
Daddy's girl growing up
Quickly, wearing blue.]

We should be grateful
We should be grateful.
Time of our savior
Should be grateful.

Can one night or a whole life
Ever be the truth?
Can one night or a whole life
Ever be the truth?

What is it that the Bible says about
The story of Ruth? Who's outside, now in
The side you choose. Which side will we choose?

Forever. – Bill's a romantic, Alice knows better.
Bill's a romantic, Alice is clever.

It frightens me, you said it frightens you.
It frightens me, you said it frightens you.

I have the answer to our concerns.
Coarsening the screw.

I love fuck you.
Love, fuck you.

...

Capture, captioned white words on black
Caption capture, white words on black

Kubrick's last words that he read back.
Kubrick's last words that he read back.

Requiem en pace, Stanley' lingering track
Classic Kubrick tale, words over music tracks
Strand of pearls on a velvet back. Velvet back.

Dream Story's Germanic playback.
UK environ takes a New York tact.

All the courtiers in the masque play.
Some are the dumbshow names get a say.

The real secret group is behind the scenes
Tech crew interjects brightest beams.

A dip of rock and roll or two to make the modern tragic.
Creates modern music, with Jocelyn's magic.

Capes and clothing to make this tale timeless.
Create a kindness, to reveal an ingenue's blindness.

The masque designers' brilliant creations
Fine-tuning their contexts with precise ablations

Of mis-en-scene and displaced visage.
Professionals not withering under demanding missives.

Spotting Arthur Jafa in the credits.
Working hard in NYC, contributing to the edits.

In the cast of characters, there are interesting surprises.

Assistant Leon Vitali's the red man, also advises.

And Abigail and Julienne we're to discern
are two different people but play one woman who got turned.

Now we see the names at the party,
Ones Ziegler wouldn't tell.
Grandest secrets now all dispelled.

The licensed music that needs to be credited
Inserted into scenes, sounds that were edited.

They even have to list the film stock he used.
Future creatives to know the celluloid hued.

Citations generated to get stuff for free
Ubiquitous product placements on film and TV

(I remember running by that Gower St. surgery, scurrying
To acting classes in last-minute hurrying.)

The very last credit with the copyright number.
To underscore Kubrick's master, in whole not to plunder.

At the tail of the moments Stanley declares "The End"
To put the fine point on the last work that he penned.

But Warners gets final word even after the director.
After **they** say we go black, they stop the projector!

Preface: Songs and Other Sevens

I came across John Akomfrah's important film, *Seven Songs for Malcom X* while I was in London researching the Kubrick archives and working on another book project. I was invited to perform at the Deptford Cinema after Melanie Abrams arranged for an event in February 2015 on the anniversary of the assassination of Malcolm X, El Hajj Malik El-Shabazz.

Viewing the film brought back many memories. I either personally knew or had met most of the commentators in the film. It also took me back to the 1990s when so many of us hoped for, assumed, that radical change was imminent. It took me back to the emotions surrounding Spike Lee's film, *Malcolm X*, and the recent killings of unarmed Black men by police that have been making international headlines.

Many of us still mourn Malcolm. He was a singular, defining figure in my family. My mother was introduced to his ideas by my grandfather. Both my grandparents were politically interested in Civil Rights causes. In addition to my grandfather supporting Malcolm X, my grandmother also supported Marcus Garvey and the UNIA (Universal Negro Improvement Association) as well as Mary McCloud Bethune. The concept of Malcolm X, writ large, how dear he was, especially to his peer group, was emphasized in the extraordinary support of Spike Lee's film (including fundraising by noted Black celebrities) but also by scathing critiques by folks who literally held him dear, such as Amiri Baraka, exemplified in his poem "The X is Black." Malcolm X continues to mean so much to Black people emblematically and intimately as a person that there continues to be discourse and controversy around him, including discussions on the extensive biography written by Manning Marable, published shortly before his death.

So, looking at the Akomfrah film, made in 1993, feels very much like experiencing the past and the present simultaneously. Akomfrah's film, as a hybrid documentary and mythology, is a beautiful creation. It also gives us great insights into the political atmosphere surrounding Malcolm X's assassination including the covert meetings that Malcolm X and Martin

Luther King were having with each other, as verified by William Kunstler in the film. The proximity of these leaders to each other, beyond the trope of their alleged animosity, was reinforced by Harlemites like John Henrik Clarke, and by Guy Johnson in comments that he made about his mother Maya Angelou's friendship with both men, during the memorial service in her honor at New York's Riverside Church 2014.

The stakes for Malcolm X's legacy are still quite high. Both he and King were an important pair of freedom fighters on par with the likes of W.E.B. DuBois and Booker T. Washington. In Akomfrah's experimental film we see the connections between many people who were influenced by Malcolm and who sought to erase binary stances about him: between his Detroit Red self (and as Robin D.G. Kelley points out, the political aspects of zoot suit culture) and his prison self; his evolution in prison and his activism in the Nation of Islam; his evolution from the NOI (Nation of Islam) and his cultivation of Pan-African American and Pan-African unity shortly before his death. These are all the same person, the same man. We see the growth of one person who encapsulated, and moved, a nation within a nation, a nation beyond a nation.

The chants created here for John Akomfrah's work is an amalgam of the two types of handholding. It is a response to a film as it's being watched. Like Kubrick's *Eyes Wide Shut* I am relying on the words and images (including images of text) as they unfold in real time viewing. Unlike Kubrick's film however, I am not relying on the viewing of Akomfrah's film to explicate the work I've written. Similar to the *Tender Buttons* commentary, "If I Re-viewed Her," "Songs and Other Sevens" is a definitive referent but stands without the source material. Unlike either of these other pieces though, this chant is primarily an erasure poem with some self-generated flourishes. In each piece I'm seeking to find a new way of playing with, understanding, exploring the idea of "handholding." I hope these explorations are evocative for the reader and listener and will cultivate a continued appreciation for this beautiful and important film by John Akomfrah.

The audio for the two versions of "Songs and Other Sevens" is available at korepress.org/TracieMorris

Songs and other Sevens

Malcolm has seven letters, a seal.
Mal-colm – Mal calm – a bad calm
Mal – colm – bad coming, a lucky number.

Detroit coming, Down from Omaha beantown, 125th.
Countryman – which country? Which man?

He had a meeting with King, with King to amalgamate causes – Kuntsler
This is true, this is true. Guy Johnson said they'd joke, over his mother's
food.

When we went there, when we went there. When we went to the
Audubon.
We went there. Billy worshipped. We went there.

The Audubon is a naturalist place. A place for nature. A natural man. A
world wonder.

It would've been a great movement. It would've been a great moment. It
would've been great. It would've been grating. It would have integrated. It
would have had integrity. It would've moved. It would have. It would have.
It would have.

At any cost. Any cost. Any. At cost. A deadly sin.

The government, the governed. The meant. The grove. He gave. Giver
governs.

The kind of expression that he had. The kind of expression. That kind of
express. That percussion. That kind. That face he had. That compression.
That day.

On his face and in his being.

We went there. We feel. Something. Anxiety. Buzzing.
How bad I make myself. How bad it makes me look.
How bad. It made me.

Look.

Face life, or death. Face death. Or or or.

I now bring before you. Before you. Before.

Get your hands out. Get your hands out.
Just then shots fired.

From the front.

Four children. Four little girls. I covered with my body.

Someone gasping. Someone can't breathe.
Something horrible. My husband.

Falling back. All hell.

Stay here. How Malcolm was doing.
He was breathing. Heavily.

All over. He was shot. All over.

Junior told the truth. Sent back to Chicago.
My tongue.

Many different Malcolms. Premiere with stars.
Black black black pinpoints in white lights.

Government is responsible. Reborn in prison.
The government is responsible. We don't need America.

Hoover. Who is Hoover and where is Hoover. Who is who?
A cretin, one of many dwarves.

Don't blame a cracker? Blacks are worse off in some categories.
Quest for a messiah.

A woman from the Caribbean, Grenada. Earl a Georgian preach.
Gregoria chanting. Noble-drew an ecstatic 7.

We were always active. We were always.
Booker T. Garvey, Earl Louise.

UNIA. Unity among people. He stayed with us. Remember that. That
Unity. Exalt.

The number of vision. His mother. Their magnificence.
She was well-educated. Politically, committed.

Being snatched awake. Our house. Our fire.
Stop saying Garvey. Compellingly, dramatic.

Not a frightened Negro. They wanted *property*.

They would harass her. They demeaned her.
They killed her husband. Ill. At ease. No one would hire.

Louise locked up. Her child locked.
Office of the state. Not a lawyer. Foster.

Pool room in Boston. Real cool. Big leg pants.
Able-bodied men who refused to war.

Able-bodies refuse to participate
Who refused war. Not refuse. Who fumed,
Who fume in suits, smoking. Flowing material and pleated
Moors in all matter, flow hair.

Konk clothes. Pleats, parted coils.
Waves on waves break. Wind blowing northeast. Billowings.

I can't wait to kill – those who done me in, killed my
Father. Draft me. I'll make a sign. Let me hold and cross arms.

One war ends. Prison Malcolm safer than on the street. A prism.
Prosser. Process. He is coming back.

Prison was a shock treatment. He may have been.
He may have been killed in that moment.

We love our people. We love. We love and we don't love.
We're non-violent. We're non-non-violent. Samurai.

Malcolm had a time with Islam. He convinced him.

I lay. I lay. I became aware. I looked.
I became aware. Suddenly he had come.

He became dangerous. He was a thinking man.
He was a threat.

Relationship with. a father image. Almost a worship.
My son. Losing his father. Losing his father.
Idols step up to get knocked down.

He worked hard. He worked. Populated.
Templed. Twenty-four and seven.

The home of revolutionary thinking.
Here, here here. Here.

Adam Clayton Powell, James Farmer.
African African African. African-American.
All continents. All climes.

Collaboration. It's 1957. King is non-violent.
Non-violence, pacifism. Destroyed by Whites.

Precinct. Renown for oppression.
Bro. Johnson was brought. He was beaten.

Malcolm brought the Nation. 2 elements.
Frenzied crowd and calm damn nation.

Harlem police were mean. Minister Malcolm
Minister Malcolm Minister Malcolm.

Thousands of people, melted, away.
No man should have that much power.

He should have had more. Administer Malcolm.
Harlem was never the same.

Government. Little, a key figure.
Minister of Temple No. 7.

He was dedicated. Recruiting.
Businesses. A paper. Animosity.

What's he trying to do?
What's he trying?
What's he doing?
What does he do?

He do, who do? He do. Who do?

Rejected gradualism. Destiny.

Changing the White man's mind.
Our own mind must be changed.

I was kind of in the middle of things.

He was the boogie man.

White man's country.
Speech. I changed. A master teacher.
Respect and love of Malcolm.
Cigarettes and liquor put away.

Complete separation. (Liberia.
Not Liberia.) A nation.

He wanted to be part because he loved his people.
Token crumbs that don't solve problems for the masses.

Destroying the system, political, economic. Destruction.

Genius of modern media. Genius politician of mass media.
Jealousy. He was a public man.

He outgrew the narrow stage. X wanted the nation to participate.
He was not given permission to be in Washington. The March.

I was convinced. If we engaged in more action.
Wherever people committed themselves. Negro Muslims should be there.

X began to see the mission of the Nation as being larger than the original
intent. He, a leader in Black America, not just, Muslim, leader.

White American leader, killed. Malcolm silenced. King coming
with Bobby.
Muslims being betrayed. Malcolm be washing dishes.

He knew he couldn't come back.
He fathered. Elijah fathered. A septuple itch.

I have the independence of action.
Immediate solution to problems confronting our.

Met peace writers of Hiroshima and Nagasaki.
Little under alias Malik Shabazz. Mecca.
Make myself authentic. Direct communication.

Establish contact with brothers on the African.
Dropping bombs. Gabriel Prosser.

African summit conference. A success.
The West African trips. John Henri(k)

Human rights, not civil rights. Not the United States,
The world. The world problem. A human problem.

Many people want to see us as the minority.
A human problem. International rather than national.
A more global point.

Connection to other Black thinkers.
3rd world countries. DuBois.
Ancient valley of Kings. Our own.
Our own problems.
The states.

You substituted Muhammeds. An idol.
Worshipping images. It's a crime.

Orders came in. Chicago.
Concern, the fruit to people who need it.

New Black nationalist organization.
I'll call you. When and where.

Organization of Afro-American Unity.
Any kind of action when we see fit.

Wire Malcolm. Wire the bomb.

Why don't you just forget it?
Let things cool off.

The Black Panther Party.
Fire prophet. Fighting.
Time has changed, power has changed.

Unusual intelligence. Learned very swiftly.
If you had something to say. Seeing all 7 oceans, seas.

European definition not necessarily **the** definition.
He had learned instantly from African leaders.

Muslim Movement was trying to kill Malcolm.
He should be. Bombed house. Elijah. Infiltrated.

FBI was aware, did nothing, or did something. Puppeteers.
Expose it. Let the chips fall. And others double-o, five-o, seven.

Wrapped in white, ready. A present.
Wrapped in white, black and white. Headlines.
Wrapped in white, ready for … rest.

Funeral at Unity parlor. Remember that word.
What he was about. Revolution.

We need someone to talk.
To talk directly to us.
Rodney King, policed
Eric Garner, policed
Michael Brown, policed
Trayvon Martin, brutality. The Law.
Where was Mark Duggan's body? The gun? Laid out.

An X. A truth teller. An unknown. A checked box.
Costs. Unvarnished, ruthless eloquent.
The analysis still valid. Memory lives.

Betty said he loved to
Betty said he loved to
Betty said he loved to
Betty said he loved. His people.
Betty said he loved.
Her love. Loves. Lover
He loves. Love you. Loves us.

Prepare for the world to come.
Prepare for the world to come.
Prepare for the world.

To come: Pre/pare: 7 Moor.

Preface to *Tender Buttons,* If I Re-viewed Her

My handholding of *Tender Buttons* began with an invitation. It was the centennial of Stein's text and I was asked, by *Jacket2*, to review it in less than 500 words in any way that I wanted to interpret the term "review."

I listened to the clip of Stein reading her poem on Picasso, a friend of hers, on You Tube. It starts with the line: "If I'd Told Him." I liked the idea of hearing her speculate on telling in her own voice. Her voice was telling.

It was also *telling*. I thought about the speculation of me presuming to review Stein. I liked the "if." Stein's voice was rather controlled, contained. It was a container. I'd just finished writing the first part of this text (or at least the first draft of it) when I was scheduled to be the opening act for the legendary avant-garde theater director and writer Richard Foreman (even though I went after him) for the Segue series at the Zinc Bar in New York in the fall of 2014. I was invited by Genji Amino whom I first met in Paris and who had begun graduate school. I was introduced by Charles Bernstein, a dear friend who had relocated to Brooklyn with his family. Charles' mother was born in Brooklyn. The reading happened to be during the Jewish High Holy days and Charles in his introduction commented that he'd always seen me, to a certain extent, as Jewish. (There is a long and somewhat comical personal history about my tenuous cultural and religious connection to Judaism, of which Charles is quite aware). It was something of an inside joke but it is also because we both have heavy New York accents which, during a particular point in NY history, irrespective of one's race/ethnicity/religion, is an amalgam of African, African-American (southern), African-American (immigrant), Puerto Rican, Irish and Yiddish Jewish. The permutations and emphases depend on where you grew up. For example Charles' New York accent has much more Bronx inflections because he went to Bronx HS Science (as my cousin Richard who grew up in Queens but has lived in the Bronx for decades, does. Charles' accent is also much more Yiddish influenced than mine, for obvious reasons.) As extensive global travelers (Charles, certainly more so than me), we are acutely aware of our accents. We've been outside of the United States often and sound more like each other, irrespective of our racial differences than, say, a Black person born in Paris or an Eastern European Jewish person born in Michigan. It's how we sound here. Despite being the granddaughter of a Rabbi, Gertrude Stein, born in Pittsburgh, sounds less like Charles, accentually, "Jewishly" than I (although I wouldn't presume to say my natural accent is at all equivalent to her cultural/religious upbringing, of course). It's a matter of inference, inflection and temporality.

There seemed to be some interesting/weird/intriguing circularity going on between Manhattan, Brooklyn, Paris. Me, Stein, Charles and Genji's invitation. The voice and performative utterances of text and how we embody it. I've listened to Stein's recording many times, so it's in my body to a certain extent.

It seemed like the right time to read the section on *Tender Buttons* that I had completed because of this symmetry and because people in the audience were familiar with much of my work already.

At the reading at Segue, I felt… something. I felt pressure. Because of Richard Foreman's presence, the room was packed to overflowing with the avant-garde literati of New York. Some of the audience members were my good friends and deep critics of art, poetics, theory, you name it. Many were kind enough to hang around after Foreman left, maybe because I'd spotted them. I felt the pressure to be present after Foreman (who is in more delicate health these days and who doesn't read in public often). I decided to read the Stein part I had written. I hadn't read it aloud before and had no idea how it would come out.

I was surprised at how it came out. It wasn't an echo of Stein's approach to the poem on Picasso; it was almost aggressive. I don't know why it was. Maybe energized by the charm of Richard Foreman's reading, maybe fear/pressure of the discerning audience, maybe a literal shout out to my friends. (At least that's how I heard it in my ears.) They, being kind friends, encouraged me to keep going with this work. This section is the result of feedback by the lovely people in that audience as well as the *Jacket2* editors who encouraged me to approach Stein's text in this way, in the first place.

⌀⌀⌀

I detected the change of mood in each portion of *Tender Buttons*. While I was sparked to respond by overarching themes and by specific words, I didn't adhere to the outlines of Stein too closely. I connected to it more as a stream of consciousness connected to the three larger sections rather than the sub-sections. My "response" to the first section was playful, exploratory, the commentary of the items of this one woman. Even if parts were not happy, they were engaged in a playful way. I was engaging with the sense of her interacting, as play, with tangible things. Things give her a sense of purpose, maybe even safety. Or they highlight how safe she *isn't*—alone, with just these things.

When I went to the "food" however, the text seemed to feel more and more distanced from the source, from Stein. I was surprised. It felt as though the muse was saying, hands on hips, "Why do I have to speak to this chick? Why isn't she speaking about my needs, my interests at this time?" As I said, I was surprised as this work came out of my hand. This "strained conversation" has more physical space, more distance, more parting of the ways than the first section did. My muse is off on her own, talking to other muses like Etheridge Knight's, my ancestors' kitchen aesthetics. The way they manifested art in kitchens at home and homes away from home (two of my mother's aunts had their own restaurants). They had a whole other conversation about food that Stein could not enter. It was about the context in which they cooked, in which cooking was done, eating was done. It was a conversation about who cooked for whom. And of course in indulging in appetites, sex is certainly entwined in the meals. This section was much more difficult to write. It continued to pull at me, pull parts of me away from other parts. Her racist epithet is also jarring and pulled me away. I was disappointed in her. (My muse was right to be pissed off at the outset. She knew what was coming…) I had more to say. It's like when you go to a garden party, a light lunch and you wear cute spring clothes, then happen to sit next to a couple of people who get into an incredibly deep discussion about a topic you're interested in. You're not dressed for that! You have to change your point of view. Your posture, your facial expressions. Your tone is not symmetrical with your dress, shoes, manicure, your hairstyle. And so you are, in a way, disjointed, off.

So maybe you make a decision to be as adorable as palatable. But it is worth it to be non-harmonious because the conversation is soul-fulfilling, cathartic, lights your brain up immediately. You forget to use the right fork after you forgot to nibble on preliminary finger sandwiches.

In each section I was pleased and unnerved by how often what I thought was a complete "riff" would segue into what Stein said next. This happened. A lot. It made me realize that one of the things that's enduring about *Tender Buttons* is how it makes you think of words that you hear/see that aren't literally present but that are in the atmosphere. Maybe that's why it was somewhat felicitous to do this project. It was just sitting there waiting in the ether, waiting for the text.

I did a significant part of this, the majority of this meditation actually, at Yaddo, the artists' colony. (I completed the writing of this entire book there.) It was a helpful environment because it elicited the salon-setting that Gertrude Stein and Alice Toklas hosted and encouraged in Paris. There was a stultified yet welcoming air among the stuffed chairs and plate-glass windows. There was also a stillness that allowed me to hear more clearly some of these words in the ether I "caught" in this process. It's the scent of wood objects, the attention to meals, the pervasive class hierarchy and romanticism about royalty that allows for this type of observation. The environment also underscored this sense of how different I was from this place and how this place has welcomed others.

One can't talk about *Tender Buttons* and **not** talk about place. The objects are placed, the foodstuffs are placed, in the rooms, everything is in place. The room is a place where things are placed.

In my food section I mostly found myself seeing food in its relationship to being outside, outdoors, the placement of things in a so-called natural habitat (not indoors). The contrast between the first and second sections is about exposure, the intent of containment while being exposed, while being outdoors.

After saying all of this, I realized, as I was completing the "Enclosed/Rooms" section that the preview to this handholding on the page began with a collaboration that Charles and I did in 2006. We decided to write a joint poem via email. (That poem, *Truth Be Told*, which also includes a short poem of mine as the coda, was published in the magazine *Brooklyn Rail* in 2010). Rooms within rooms, screens within screens, time within time.

This conversation with Stein, her musings and my muse. Her inflections on Picasso and my reflections on her, is typical of how artists make work. We make each other. We view, review, view.

The audio for "If I Re-viewed Her" is available at korepress.org/TracieMorris

If I Re-viewed Her
Objectively,

If I reviewed her, if I reviewed her. I reviewed her. Her her button. Her boutonniere. Herbal. Her boobeleh. Her boo. Her Too. Her tuchas. Her view. Her book.

If I viewed her like I used to. I talked to. I teased her. I teach her. I reach. I rearview.

"If 'if' was a fifth…" Black lettres. Black pov. "res" onate. Ur-words. Sona. Salon. If I revved up, I could view her through another glass, Toklas, another poem. W(h)atts a smatter-shattering. That piece of bright bling attached to a cloth with sharp edges,
rounded o'er time, a button. A carafe.

What patterns clash? What suits ya? What cymbals? What Sabians, Armenians, Jews, Germans, Blacks, Latins, Americans? Euro-detritus? Ex-plights' us? I wonder.

The "gratitude of mercy" is not explained. Isn't made plain. The nose on your face, lalala vie en rose. What colors rise? Vie(w) finder the size of a nickel. A dime, the side of it, is the side of a button, the way it hems the pocket. The way you finger it. The pointed nature.

Blood in the face. Blood on the leaves. It's a violet hue. It shifts from blue. White gold. A shift is a ditty dress. Dirty is yellow at points. Whitest whites not coal-colored. Not coal. What's matter? A large box clocks handily. It cloaks. When I do count the clack that tells what I re-sign to be, ore no (t).

Lilies are white unless tiger, unless striped. Unless (la) t (i) tude. Un-less and un-still, etude. What's the sound in that box? What kind of box is it? Harmonica, piano, coffin, shoo? Masque of red. Of Venice, of revenge, of reverb. The purpose of a box is to let things bounce around inside, not out. They're all maracas, all boxes, all cojones. And that is why there (they) aren't brass. They're bells and open at the bottom. Like a review.

Stepping up to the plate to review is base. It is the ground. It's dirty. It's around. It's cutting corners like sports for war. It's saying pen's mightier: a tool, a gourd. Assessments are objects. Alchemical and base.

2.

At the bottom is Jimmy Cobb in Miles' kinda color. Chambers' music from an engorged lighting in a bottleneck. The fretting comes plaited, the strings curve around the fingers S, a female shape. A dress. A Tiffany lamp, a vamp to attest, to a taste. Petit for-fours.

A swallow bubbles. Bubbles up words. Polite Tourettes'. A set of words water the mouth. They are things that take shape that glide down the throat. Taken (a)back, tobac. A carbo-nation, a turbo-nation turn. The bubbles, Brooklyn circles sweet simple syrup. Another slender needle.

A recording. These pieces of a house of hers. Her work, her dust, her… polishing. The dark places gleam in this paper stock card house and its phoneme particles across the board. A rainbow.

Places to go red again, wheelbarrow. Another poet who knows how a black comb can be placed in the hair, how the sun sets in the wide Caribbean sea after-raining. How brilliant colors are the state of things when the daily clouds are not dark grey. The "too ra loo ra loo ral" relocate. Green as red blend in.

A blue coat is not a red coat in this regard. A blue coat is bluer and a red coat redder.

The grey is Tin Pan Alley's. The percussive keys, New York. There is not the softness the name implies but the black and white holds up. Color? That quick rhythm. The 88 lucky numbers one hope one hits. Dark custom and no greyscale. A hardened snapshot, snaps shut.

A bedspread, a throw. A throwaway line. A carved grapevine on a chair's feet in a drawing room. An appointed room. The man with the scythe flutters the veil. More dark custom. The facts of dark matter. The wake. This is a show, a showing. Having a seat and muted tones, tea. Scones. Dirty dishes and crumbs. After all this. After all this, heartache, this bruise, she has to do the washing too. After she sits.

After she breaks down.

They hand envelopes to the bride. She goes around around in white. Puts them in her purse. Why don't they do that at the other service? That's when she'll need it. That's when she'll need it. All she has in it: keys, lipstick, handkerchief. Small hard things, lace. She needs a crinoline in there, wrapped by a rubber band.

She holds the handle. It's raining. Grey tears. Masque, mascara. The day replaying over suds, over seltzer, overlays. Mother of pearl handle. White hunter's animal horn also mounted by him. Her mounted by him. The pallbearers pick him up. Both he and she are lighter. She might have been pulled up by the wind on this grained day. Streaks on the photo. She wipes.

Grape leaves, grapes stems. This motif. A universal.

A drink. Bottle, cup, glass. This earthenware variety for different means. These belongings. These things she squeezes.

She sees. She swings swigs liquid the color of rain. She mends it. Brittle papier-mache. Construction. Card. A tree sliced thinner than cake. Still life th(r)ough. (knock would)

Origami, with eyes. Markers, crayon, wax. A seal of something. A promissory notation. A jot. Drops dropping. Still wearing her coat. Deciding.

Under that coat, a coat. Under that black, white. She is in between coats. She's a prism. A triangle of a waist. The scythe, the window. The fire.

The sandwiches on the saucers, crustless. Mayo spreads and spreads, indistinguishable from porcelain.

Dotting the eyes daintily. Petals to the casket, the survivor. An unconscionable hue under the circumstances. A hint of a color.

A Werther's a peppermint under the circumstances. A grandmother, a girl. An inheritance of her heir. What's she got to give? Hard sweets now. In her eyes, a crinkle.

This one's hair is colored. It's a crinkle around her hat. "Tight curls." Springs up like flowers defying gravity, the grave situation. A maid to the other lady, lays the body in the sateen. Two women. A cohesive.

Brown skin and porcelain. Salon under uncertain circumstances. Both waiting. Antoinette, Jane. Where's Jean? Sun and grey make steam. Make rainbows, sips tea.

Pauline, saltine. Watermelon crackers. Watermarks, salt deposits, street smarts. Street sweepings over graves. Someone shutters. Who gets a rise out of whom?

An uncomfortable silence, an expectoration.

Elbows placed on a table. A scene. Mesa blanca. Ectoplasm in a glass lens. Chemical processing. It did shake. Shook it.

They shooed it when it shook. They eschewed it. It was fake. Pus, hence the handkerchief to the face.

Pero, perrito slakes. He curls under the table by the shod feet of those two. Smells rosewooded grapes.

Grapes at the wrist. A delicate glass is picked to the lips. Canine settles in.

Brown eyes level, minstrelly.

Blackening up, formerly used for furniture. If she can read… not furnishing. Not.

And this new Black, this newsprint, this ink on the apron, bleak. Bleak cleaning. Red all over.

The throw on the chair becomes a shawl, became shy, covered shoulders that shutter. Stole. As he did. An erress? wraps the hollow up at the fringe.

The edges of frayed pages in this view. In this mediumship, in this penman. This vaulted environ.

Suppose suppose I told her, even after her repose? A typed pen silvered o'er borders on black glass where she rests.

These bronzed digits typing. I watch them take form from key strokes like a piano. The mechanisms for making, unseen. A space between utility and instrument. The hearing in the ear, a scratch of tapping nails, covered up.

The joints. The natural arthritic laying on of hands to generation. A poised angularity to, to message.

Inside the peeled pencil is dark grey. Black Took letters and lead astray point of viewing. Commentate.

Black pixelate from a brown house. An address. A crackerjack to munch. Apprise inside.

Room with a review to let.

Consumption;

Roasted toasted, the beef you got, the chops. The swig and swing. The
sweet. Black coffee, brown sugar, the black berry. Lactate and effect,
an ovum, several Eve's fruit. The asp, the tale, the fault of her, the split.
The spit, the barb, the loin. Swim in that water, the euphemis, dermis,
the crush, the cakes, the onion, that back, those eyes of spuds, the stud,
the color of black as baked goods, as snacks. That season tan, the bland
sameness, for fun we lay down on blankets, with baskets, cured meat
delicacy, tube steak toothpick, celery, crudités, vegging out, raw stuffs,
a tart sauce. A bird, l'orange, the smoothness. The absence of friction.
Everyone likes eating, everyone wants a taste. The clarity in a broth, a
brothel, the exchange. The appetite. The list. The understanding. Money
and barters under a table.

I look and look at lists of "oo" and salivate. I gravitate. I vegetate toward
the tasty. I t-t-t in my buds in my glands, the glissando of "ahh" when I
remember oohs and what they were like on the tongue's tip.

Whassup? Whas' yo beef? Why you flexin'? Who made you chief? Where's
this bull from the catastrophy of lost buffalo, in the heat. That beef tip still
roasting among the Ins.

In the inner inner of this this land's bounty is plenty of charred flesh
churascuro, too ral loo real: bbq is a black boy sammich, strung out,
tressed tied and folks lick lips saying sir, loin. Don't sleep on that, don't
sleep, on the outside there's a reddening alright and flames too, and flames
do ring around the rosey and who gets those now, the buffalo cultivators
pose that's who.

There's their mountain. There's there to do. All that food they made all
that brocade had to come from somewhere. The curtains, Scarlett Oh and
throwing her ooh shade.

The side neckening, the reckoning, on Scarlett's kin, the kind of morsely Miss Anne thrope. A trope of taste. A dean, a Pall, a pox rocks blackened fish getting a collab on: Native and salmon like my Gran, ginger and chocolate like her gran, we got the whole cookie culture range in my fam. Forrest was right about chocolate boxes, enough sweets in the larder and all the colors get hankering: from my tamarind sugar mix, my brother's jasper variation, first cousins' flambéd maple. Same ultimate untimely. Shadows of different play.

No pause in that action, still fretted notes, worried, gliss tremolo in a jazz standard in a big. What's the whoop-de-do? It's the feel, kinda. I know you hear him in that background, that black, that black and tan, that Bobby Bland in the audience of magenta, indigo on stage, that relay. The subjective ding-ding. That tinny.

Tinnitus is when you can't turn it off when that sound one is grasping at, that four-eight foray, that triple quarter, its delay is being chased. Chased like a diamonic cast in a McQueen flick – either Steve. (I recognize characters.)

Trunks steaming of a getaway train, early stages post-coast, slowly up the mainline of the great migration. What's this got to do with victuals? Why the preface? Who do you think puts out the tablecloth, presses it? Spit-shines your glass in the café car? Tucks your linens tight, whitens your whiteness.

You right though, this is a premise to something delicious, a shit-less punchbowl. Crystal of the manor-born. The fatback one chews on under the matter, under the stairs, in the bodega that puts out the fruit you select as bruise-less. Who do you think gets dis colored?

These colored. A little soft shoe on sand, the glassy-eyed piper, the shim-sham Sammy Junior. He didn't know his station, he didn't know, wouldn't go for it, not limited to kith & kin. Ah well, very. He was slim. Skin reflective, showing scenes and self, An American mirror. Salted the earth, with kit, with Britt.

He remines, of something, someone. My greats, my grands, migrants, A sister daintily uses tongs to serve white bread. She wears a hoop skirt, curls around her ear. Betty Boop was Black all kewpie lips, hip dysplasia and order of the garter, her counting ways, her dance. The green collar around the drake jewel. A circular down comforter.

Very I sing. I sing heartily of EK's shine I. Better than to be dragged down to the sulfur, beginning. Shine singing damn near on earth not at sea. Cuts up obstruction. A resumption for him, a resurrection, a swim. Dirt, nap.

Shine's Adam. Shine's apple. The difference being. Plain. And plantains. The thicker skin to peal. Laughter around a whip, a picknig. We eat make food, unconsumed. Full bellied laughter. All lung.

Easy to exchange laughter, people. I mean to change people. I mean to exchange people. To count people like change based on difference. What difference did it make? Back then, back then to change to count on it was to fraction. Each person the same, a fractal of the case. The majority of fifths. The flatted foot caught running.

Tapping a leg, a bottle. A jig, a jug. Thick blanket in a meadow cutting a delicious. Cutting meat, making piecemeal of sheets, blankets, blackened people. I remember. I know that's not what she's saying. I know this is not what she says. I know what I'm saying. I know the expectorate, the expectation of what she says and I'm saying: another piece to digest, to ingest, to infer. Who put what in that basket you're swinging? What's swing? Your hand is. One side is thick-skinned, the other is languid. Some are ladylike with hats. Had hats big like baskets. Bad. There's a division. A cleaving a cleft at the center, at the neck. Tender, better, all together.

Considering the circumstances. Considering them. What was happening then? Where were we? Who are *we*? You. Artful. An arched brow. A bowed back. Fruit bowl, flies. Someone is tending to the kids there, romping under the swing, the swinging, the swung. Seeing a bee sting, saying ow. Someone is under a blanket pollinating here, here and here. Now, not now, now. That piece of meat is delicious. Roasting, basted. How many here tasted it, what is wafting in the air? That flavor. Most of our buds are in our nose, bound. In those sandwiches, in the potato salad, the napkins. The sliced melon on a hot hot day. Considering the circumstances I'm surprised at how hot a day it was. Hotter for others. Is that jasmine? Is that Jasmine? In the circumstances it could be. It could be Eula or eucalyptus. It could be magnolia or Marjorie. Margarine in the sandwiches. A migraine in that confection. A head aches. An allergy. The pollen swirling among the flowers. Was that Polly? Pauline? A saltine and Saul. Head bowed didn't save him. Weeping did. Head lower at a jaunty angle. Angel under. The circumstances.

A kind of control, a bird. A kind of perch. Each pigeon, a carrier, praying for a dot dot dot. 01 praying that the babe doesn't favor the host of the occasion. 1 oh praying the babe isn't taken. They sit in contrast, the same. One working, one pretending to play. In the play a gift wrapped up in string among the tastes, the watercress, that crease. Saying she was overtook, black took overtaken. She had to say it to be in good company, this que. The tip off. He hid. Hat's off, his head. A formal affair. A necktie party. The glare of one bird to another over glazed over eyes. Over ham.

Nothing precious, a gift to her. To spend, to thrift. A party for social acceptance. Waiting for two in the bellie. One forced, one frayed. Both waiting. Pass the affection. The cake. He split it. A spit. The trunk. The splinters the weight. At the pelvis yes and off the shoulders. Diaphanous. A lightening. Fireflies shakes her shoulders prettily. Ask for lemonade after meat-eating. She's parched from the fanning, the heat. There is a ladle and the ice turns, cools, becomes slimmer, tender. It swirls. The bitter and the sugar. The glistening. A contrast to the red, the bodied. This is a light affair.

A man doffs his hat, spoons translucence. A good egg. He's wearing a feather. He fans her.

How many times and places has this play played out? Under a myriad of miriams? A circumnavigation of doffing, ladling, a smile. Grateful girls of a certain moment, hoping to still have it. Munching with a man over a meal, trying not to eat too voraciously, not seam to hungry. Tasty but don't taste to mu(n)ch. Don't be testy, desperate, left. A universal. Teeth, taste, state, status, doesn't matter. Isn't relevant. The waiting to be picked, helped to forego for helping. To get what's left and like it. Grateful and great. That's how women do it. Men deign.

Why do we take it? This uneven display. The unfairness, the fake, the array? We don't need or eat it. We take in. We play. Where's the leftover sent away to. Awetu. A weight too.

Long purples, hoar leaves. Daisy damsels are not even with other women. Who the plates go to. The leftovers, that remains.

[Cultural interlude: The vibrato of the second fiddle, to Laertes, Polonius, H., Gertrude, a ghost. Ghosts seem to get all the play, Big H(up), Yorick, Pops, me. A girl with flowers. An expediency. How long are we to trill, to ripple? A grown woman like G. Taking me off his hands, her offing me, her offering. Me with a bastard bun, me looking away from the ghost. In fairy and in plays, in the playing of real life, of still life. The distilled in the tree, I am waiting. A lady. Waiting to be next, either wait or get burned like him. What is it with these men and their dark, furrowed brows? Their black coverings? Their inevitable ending?]

At the hands of state power, unenviable death. Hanging, poison, the spear, the fire. The state burns you. Affiliate cooties and the state sates itself in ashes. I'm ashen, blood leaving my face. Drunk with power. The drink, the pearls. In the glass, around the throat. Pearls on a ribbon. Hides bites, the snares, burns.

How Victorian, how tied up. The joy in weakness, success, symmetry in opposites. My whiteness, my witness of the whitest. His darkness, his depth, the darkest. There are two kinds of ghosts: ectoplasm and absence of it, of space without light. That place before lightness asserted itself. That was what was enforced: reflected beauty, brilliance, the glare that b(l)inds, (b)links. A ruby.

How Victoria. What Price? What is the use of the senses, their fate? Their spell? Their smell. Light and color don't have one. Not money, not like the book says. Love me nots either. A detection, like hearing that you cannot

close, you cannot cover. It hovers and tells you where you are. Everyone
smells bated breath. A liar.

A break:
A seat on the fainting couch. A sprall. One enters an empty subway car
at one's own risk. One enters a boxcar at one's own risk. Fear of being
trapped, something being drawn out. Scotts to Sunnyside. Boros, borders.
Waft and heft, detection.

It wasn't Saturn's day, it was Odin's. It was a day of harvest, it was a power
move. In the prime, at the beginning of fertile years. Just in spring.
What choices Friggs made. What a difference a day/dame makes, mate.
Chattering, not an equal division.

Anyway. Anyway. Any way. It doesn't matter. Let's move on. Let's move on
with our lives. Those who have lives, half lives. Move on with it. Any way,
at any rate. The going rate, Vicky's. Going, going. Gone.

To be older. To not get older. There's only one way to not get older. As you
age in prism, time passes but does not pass. Passes you buy. There's only
two ways Black boys die. They age and age out. They age-apropos. Those
who appropriate. The agency. It's not a suction. It's an auction. They were
not dirty, they were cherubic. Then they went in. They all went in. They
went all in. They went. Everything said in this paragraph about young
sheep, colts, erasure. Difference is. The statute. The limit of the lambs.

The banging of the gavel is a sound. Banging is a sound. It's order. It's over.
It's resounding. A bell chimes dinner.

There were choices when they were bonin'. Little boy bones, exploring.
There was a sound the girls cried and that sound was heard for miles. Even
taken back, taken aback, talkin' 'bout. There was banging in the room
they couldn't hear. They were in a room they didn't know they were in.
The room got smaller, smaller. One of them in the room, in a smaller and
smaller room smelled toast. What does that mean? What was browning?
How did the shadow get there? It's getting longer, it's getting darker.
The sun is setting in a car, a box, a car, a box, a room, a box, a shadow,

a box, a beating, a box, a fight, a box, a sunrise, a box, a sunset, a box. Schoedinger's colored cats.

Black cats aren't lucky even if it's night. Their glowing eyes give them away. They can't stay in shadow squares ever. Not even with a flashing smile, not even with gold teeth. Not even, with smooth skin, not even being a kitten. Not even purring. Not even after someone pulls them up by the scruff. Where are they landing me after they Frisbee?

"Plymouth rock landed on us." We were eating. We were snacking. We were looking for things. We were on our way up north. We were casting nets and became fish. We were casting nets and became the fish's food. We were casting nets and in our broad arms, in what looked like hammocks, in what rocked like a cradle, we were gathered.

We were scooped. We were a ladle. We were in a soup. We were spooned but not spooning. We were curled but not cuddling. The saliva in our mouths curdled in sea spume. And that's why our teeth rattled. Each tooth. One by one. We were in something shaped like a smile but we weren't grinning. No matter what they say. When they put the bit in we were not smiling. When they put the yoke on, we were not pastoral.

Heavy heavy iron and steel in the sun. When they took off, when they took that off, red red. I mean **red** red red. I mean the reddest. Red. I mean, the reddest part of you that could conceivably be from black. I mean "Who said black is a baser hue?" with that kind of red? **No** one could say that. No one could see that after seeing that color. We see that color every day in our eyes. Even the eyes under water are that red. The red expands in their tunnels, the red expands in their corridors. By the time the red stops being red, it's the grosser name, it's long purple. It's red and blue. It's black and blue. The browning has browned all the way to grey and that grey becomes a *rey* of purple. Bluer than any black.

Seeing us all those colors (only) I wonder if they ate us. I wonder, if there was another reason we were roasted. I wonder what Leopold hosted? Why'd he burn the evidence? What I'd like to see Conrad write about: the heart, the heartlessness. What did they do with it? How'd it taste? I mean, if we were chattel. If they were cackling. If they were as crackled as the prepackaged snacks in store. Like the scalping, like a head scratched clean off, they said the Reds did, they did against Red. Against red. A contrast. A ghost. I wonder what they ate? I wonder why they talk about Aztecs like that? I wonder if they are saying something again? Something in ink again? Something about Incans? About the spilling.

When we brought food, despite our emaciation, despite emancipation, we brought foods. Black foods. They had foods, Red foods. I wonder. I wonder. I wonder what they'd do without our colored foods: watermelon and tomatoes. Red fruits full of water, spilling.
/break over

If I had to review her, if I had to rewind, if I had to redo, reuse, renew… I'd think about where those foods come from. She know? I'd wonder how they'd get full. I'd wonder if what we did with pig parts of necessity, they did to us out of luxury. The abundance of us growing in the fields.

Except on Saturday? Except on Sunday. When Saturday turns to Sunday we pray. It was regulated. We weren't working because we were working. We weren't working because we were working up a sweat. We were working and sweating on Sunday. We were swaying. A cold sweat. A thirst.

In any way to be older was a blessing. To be a loader was a blessing. To tote was a blessing, a mote. We are smitten. We smote, we smoked. Our hair turning grey, our skin turning, turning on a spit. That smoke that hangs in the air. They were full of it. The air was full of our surface. As we sat smoking, they were surfeit on the surface. In any age, in every way.

The crackling is a sound. A cracker sound, a fire. Fat, black and cackling. The women, as their women, pretended. As they turned any witcha way, smelling the dry roasting, the cinder and shame of that party. The breaking wood, weeping willow, bone, ash, birch, jacaranda. More purple.

How small one gets without the fat. Rooster becomes pigeon. Guinea hen becomes game hen. Cooking calcifies, makes smaller. Distance between electrons, Adams, is infinitely smaller. Cartesian halves, Zeno trope.

Two points joined, make a joint. Make a shadow. It looks 3 dimensional, loosely. A loosening of a dimension, of light. What is a sculpture? How do we know it when we see it? Because of the light play. Because of the way light shines off of it. Because of the shadow. Because of the shadow, this loose playing of the "facts" of the matter. The way it shatters a prism. That's what it's loosely based on. So when they call us shadows, when they call us spooks, spooky what they're saying is, what they're saying is that we are what is reflected off them. They are *repleat* with reflections. Everyone else is just a mirror, a mole. A collection of melanin, potential melanoma. Sambo is samo. They say simian = Indian = Black. In the dark who knows, among the grey, who cares? In a colonial, a colony is a colony. And so the same stories are. It's what is killing but can be unseen. On the underside of people. Which we are not. In which way we are not.

So we are like, the opposite of light. The lightness of being. Garnet, ocre, brick, midnight all variations of a spectrum, a prison. That's how we're seen, refracted. White becomes the bone, and the marrow. The hardest part at the core. Calcium is more than a trace mineral, it's the base. It's not ash or dust. It's not sand or iron ore. It's a kind of powder.

And what of marrow, real marrow. Marrow that's the colors. All the colors, all the cells. What do we do with that? Sweep it under. Whatever's left we water down. Make into soup. When we're in a stew, in a pickle. When we're in stasis, then they say, See? We're all the same here. Root stock =/= the chef's match stick. The one who lights the pilot.

Hope is a thing. Feathers are a thing. Feelers are a thing. Hope abstraction? Is it only for some? Is it a luxury? Is it an economy? Is it a treat? Is it a trap? Is it payback? Is it slacking? Is it Black? Is it smacking? Is it gummy? Is it chewable? Is it lewd? Is it laudable? Laughable?

Tin is a poor man's pewter. Pewter is a poor man's platinum. Platinum is a poor man's grapheme. Grapheme is a poor man. Women don't have mettle. Women are golden globules.

Coal is the goal of diamonds. Diamonds want to go back, they don't want to be stuck. They're not amber. Amber likes stillness Amber lives in trees.

Coal is the color that is the blackest. It's the deepest earth. It's the top of liquid fire. It's the molten cover. When coal becomes hard, and cold it is a diamond. So if coal **is** a color what are we saying about each other?

We we ain't sayin' it are we? We ain't saying it? We don't claim it. We **say** we are saying it but we're saying something else. That else is what we prefer to talk about. It's what we want, what we waste, it's more "tasteful." It's blasé, it's flam*based*. Delicious in our mouths. Not hot too long.

Goodness = gracious. Gracious = elegant. Elegant = lovely. Lovely = hospitable. Hospitable = welcoming. Welcoming = accepting. Accepting = inoffensive. An inoffensive woman is a good woman. This woman knows the rules.

She gets got. She gets gotten. She gets to be a she. She gets. She gets it.

I don't get it. I don't even know. I'm not even known. I'm not even grown. I'm knot even. I'm. I'm 'Chaim. I'm open in the back of the throat. That's what eye c.

Please be the ___. I want the ____. I don't eat the _____. I am the vehicle for it.
It goes right through me.

I'm a negligee. Clearly.

I'm a Teddy. I'm not a growler. I squeak. That's what they say. This is not about me eating or being eaten really. It's about a flounce at the bottom, an opening at the top.

If I'm ____, I'm (a) very low cut.

Hell. I'm a bargain.

2.

}:
Please please please please. [refrain]
Please please please please. [refrain]

Please [ahhh oooh oh oh oh] please.
[the other line]

Mercy. Mercy. [pronoun]: everytime I think I'm outtie,
I'm an innie. I'm cordial. I'm slim. I'm a chickadee, serif, sirrah.
I'm Girlie, curlie. I'm under the ground. I'm knotted. I've got a
Binding on me. I've got a hidden agenda. I'm tied to a
Stick with a not. I'm knot sayin'. I'm just [verb].

Cloudiness at eye level is fog. Mist at knee level is mystery.
Clouds at toe level is dewey. Kinds of haze.
The deweys are at all levels.
Once gone, they don't come back. You just never know.

Sooner or later. Sooner **or** later. Soonerorlater. A schooner.
A schlong, a jerk. A baller. A jag, a jackboot. Jaded. A blue jay.
A bracera, a banana. A bathtub, a boy, a biota. Sooner or later that
Boy will become a man. He'll be taught to be a man. He'll be
Manageable, man-handled. A handler. He'll have greatness thrust.
Sooner or later.

He'll try it.

He'll say what he is told. He'll do what
He is told. He'll be told to.
He'll get old being told what
To do, how to do it. He'll be screwed.

He'll do the screwing. He'll be a bulb.
A round base, a skewer.
He'll be a screwdriver. He'll be driven.

He'll be a driver. He'll have the privilege **if**

He decides to do what
He's been told and re-tell it:
(Er…ver(s)acity,
what's intended, ruditement)

He'll do well if
He recites it.

If he's a certain kind of he. If he isn't a he like a "hee-hee" he, a "haw
haw" guffaw, He'll have problems. He'll project them onto others. Others
problems will be pro-Jected onto him. And then there's trouble. No matter
what or where the matter is, it'll be about him. Hm.

(It'll shift and it'll be shitty if he doesn't resell/retell that ditty. Goes
something like: "Yo ho ho." That's not begging. That's not saying please or
mercy. That's a declarative.)

And that's how it went on how it goes on. How do you say? "Breaka
dawn"? That's how it's said (by some). And yes, bi-some is how it ends
(rhymes, rhumes). It ended here with bison. With the end of them. That's
where the lordly gave some beef and took some away. Red took. Can't say
"too much" (infinite blood streams, still counting 'em).

The coagulate is cold in red took, black too. All the colors in the blood, in
the deep meat. In gristle, cartilage, fat. Black red taken, dislocated. At this
joint. Cooked.

(Where is all that coffin from?)

3.

With that old ass word, with that old ass man. The age of "old ass" is
undetermined and undeterred. It's the age of math. It's a primary language.
The primordial language is poetry. The prudent language is poetic

language. Poetics isn't shadow, it's liliacs (a flower and an allergy) isn't detritus, isn't extra. Poetics is seeds, from which tender shoots exclaim/ MH Abrams. It's the first utterance and the second saying is math. One word plus another. One sound then another. The joining of the call of the response is divine, divination, mathematical and poetic. Poetry is the first and the last. It's

Which came first what we said or what we heard?

The muttering or the mutterer. The mutton or the lamb. The expression is funny. It doesn't say "hen" or "egg" (in the usa) we say chicken. We can't wonder female first. We can't entertain it in entertainment. We neutralize sex, say "chicken." We can't say it (t)hen.

Spermatozoan homunculi are still floating around in situ, in lingo. In ga(u) ge. In our hope for the human. Always male, an avatar. The chef? Yes. The chef. Before the chef, the chief. The chief that made the quickening. Master of all he surveys.

His kids watch and they all learn something. How to earn it. How to make it. Make the mutton. Girls mutter and bake. Boys roast, take. Some boys. Some boy already ate.

One hand holds, the other hand steadies. Teeth pull, tear, masticate. In a vestibule, juice dribbles. They laugh. More juice dribbles. People clean, off plate. Those people are the other people. They're the other people because they dribble, different dribbling. There's more than one way to. Depending on how you do it, how well you do it, how it's done, innately or no. Depends on who's eating, who got served. Who's full. Who gets the leftovers. Whose the leftovers. Who gets and who gets it.

Those who get it give shade, are shades.

Tight curls are highly curled. The looser, the better. The tighter, the loser. Curls are the inverse of better. How one wears big ringlets. How one blings iron rods, hot irons.

When a hot comb pulls curls. When a hot comb, when hot rods get so
close to flesh they rake it, they bake it. When it pulls off, say, in the hot
sun, Under the sinking, pinking shears. To pink it. To put the pinch under.
Blood coarsening. Of course. Rows of curls are a coarse.

An eye, an eye. An eye minus an eye. An eye plus an eye = Ice.

What does it mean to melt? What does it mean that too too solid flesh
could melt? I mean, have you ever seen it? Have you ever seen flesh smelt?
Under what conditions, under what fire to liquidity? Membranes unpuff
something become plasma. What that screwed Shylock? States of matter.
The technicality. Isn't flesh. Flash fry: Fat.

[Rhetorical typing: Why "Black folks =/= swimming? Ratio of muscle
to mass? Fat ass ain't gristle, it's muscle. When Black are cooked on usps
cards, incinerated muscle shown off. Black muscularity in mind. In Othel
words, who they are. Swimming in corpulence. Our muscle torn from
bones, heavy lifting. Overworked. That's what they found at the Afam
burial. All flesh doesn't melt. Well cooked, it falls off, tender(ed).]

So much is about the surface. The superficial, the serenity it causes. A cloth,
a kind of clothtrophobia. There's the seed and then there's the surface. What
we define as something is something that comes through the surface or
something that is waiting to break the surface. We don't describe it as the
thing that is not superficial. We see a seed for what it's waiting to be, not
what it is. Flesh is what we see. Triglicerides by the surface. We see skin on
top. Not layers. We don't see skin as a depth thing except what breaks it.

And this is where mud comes in. Mudders, muddy boots, mud halls? You
know it's more than top. Mud is not the tip but the insides. Mud is the
inside, out. Egyptians love lotuses. (It was blue. Wouldn't you be?) They
are the mud. When you dig. When frogs dig. When the water digs itself.
What's in the water checks itself, out.

A lotus is an exclamation, a lotus is a proclamation. It's food for thought.
It's food food for herons, humans. It's something else for Buddha, Krishna's
eye, a non-blue variety.

Someone **could** eat something blue but how often? How likely is it? Besides the purple berries closer to the sky on the spectrum but not really. Not in nature. There's dyes and indigo, an indication. A proflagration. A migration. A blue lotus, A bluing. A caduceus could be the beginning of a lotus. A couple petals. The ascension of the first two.

Herons eat the smaller bones, the finer points, the details in miniscule. Heroin eats the arteries, the arterioles, the capillaries. Heroines eat nothing. They are self-sacrificing. They are consumed, consummated, summa consommé.

They are often a mealy-mouthed meal. Usually saying something breathy, usually breathing to cool the soup. So that some else can eat. Someone meatier.

What does it mean to break? What does it mean to break, fast? Heroines stay out of the way. Heroines don't make a break for it. They break. Usually a leg. While running from a monster. What makes them a heroine? Two things: they say, "Don't save me" they = get saved, the hero can hero.

The hero eats a hero so the hero can be a hero. She makes a hero to make him the hero. She's not quite a hero. She's a hero with a feminine syllable, two feminine rhymes. So not a hero hero. She's the dot-dot-dot kind. The ellipses kinda. The one that drags.

She breaks early but not fast. She has to break first so he has the meal. She doesn't eat, she makes. That's what **they** say. No him, no problem. That's what she says, her too.

She is sick of shining. She is sick of cleaning. So she doesn't do it. Get take out. Then take the trash out. Take your ass out, she says. She says it to her and they both say. What are **you** doing here?

Know what doesn't need a plate? Pizza and watermelon. Messy but expected. What you **need** with those is napkins, cloths. Plates aren't apropos. Indecent, depending.

3.

Loving tongue and pepper. When she says that she means it. When I hear
that I mean, I see somethings. I see something in particular. Gefilte, lox.
I see them on a plate. Sometimes creamed onions. Sometimes bagels. Of
course coffee. They all go together in/on porcelain or plastic. You know the
color. The default to keep it all crisp. They always go together. They always
go. Go they tell them. Go scram.

It's not easy to put it all together. It costs. A colored loss.

Anyone can become colored if someone wants to pursue it. The more
wanted, the more porous, unporcelain.

The tub, the sink, the radiator, got it covered. Same cover, different stains,
paints. The first food should be in a sunny room, a room full of light, heat.
Hella light, helium. The lightest. That's what it's binding to, the lightening.

Sunny side up, separation of yolk from the translucent, the shell. It just
slips out. It just slips on a griddle. It was meant to be eaten. It's way too
easy.

It slides out with a crack.

Into batter, into butter, into a mouth, into a month. The same thing.
Always welcome, whether mixed up or not.

Whether on a crust or in a crust, whether crustless or crustfull. Whether
crested or crestfallen. Whether undercooked or ashy. Always welcome.
Always ready to go with something, even itself. Like mayo, marshmallows,
tofu, certain cheeses, white rice and breads. The mildness, the absence of
much there makes everything else sing. Makes you appreciate the other
things. Makes you grateful.

It's an answer, if not a remedy, like the weather. Something we all, most
normal people, have in common. It's a wise crack.

A regular color is translucent. It's "unaffiliated." It's neutral. It's "natural." Everything else isn't essential. So they say… and most of us mean "we" when we say "they." It doesn't make juice, it's the absence of juice. It's water. Cocoanut water. Bathwater. Rosewater. Porcelain ablution.

There's this weak-day kind of water that this is. The bath that one takes before getting out there, in the work world, whirling down the drain. You need breakfast before heading out to work. Just to get ready to head out there. Watching it swirl down prepares you for what your day will be like. It's a wending, a staircase, a funnel. It's funny. It's weft. A common theme. Something to work with.

Being late is no excuse. Eating is no excuse. The traffic is no excuse. The transportation is no excuse. Waiting is no excuse. There's no excuse not to be here. To not exude enthusiasm. To not talk about anything that isn't work-related. To not related anything to not work is not related. There's no excuse. There's no cue. There's no ex. There's only cause. The cause is to work one's way towards it. And by "it" he means "me", meaning him. Singular.

You are in a sorry state. An unstrange state. The typical state. You are satiated and how can you have any say? No saturation for you. No fulfillment. I like the hungry look. This is a quotation. They had a quorum and agreed to the quote. There were literally four. Not "literally" literally, dictionary literary, which they rote.

Keep you on edge of the plate. The lip of it. You could be on the lip or you could catch the crumbs. Up to you, he says. Intention, indentation. You look over the lid and say, push it to the edges, I'll lap it. Insightful.

Hot under the collar. Winsome. Lovely. Don't get too comfy. Hard benches, the munchies, hard seats. Even on the day off from the workday, working. Posture. Hand in gesture. You always have to answer to somebody. The brink, rim, border of your seat, plate, bed.

Even the tub is embroidered, the small clawed feet.

You try to remain sweet. That's what everyone said you should do.

People who say money isn't important have money or something people want money for, like water. They want plenty. They don't want to have to worry. That's what they want. Lots of it.

A lot: where you put your plenty. A lot means plenty of pecks.

A lot can be divided. It can be separated. Muchness is an aggregate but measurement is another form of math. Math and accrual is not a universal language even though many would say so. A collection of work is not a product, not a production and not always food for thought. It can be something that is laid on top of a thought, laid on top of a truism, laid on top of a rumble. The rumble can be a maid, can be made from something already made. Can be whipped into shape.

That'll put you in a pickle, that'll put you in a stew. Might get you stewing. Might bet you steaming, if you're the maid and or if you're whipped. If your shape is whipped.

Into a frenzy, into a lather, into a froth, into a merengue, into a batter. By a batterer, by a battering ram. What's a sprinkle?

Is there **a** sprinkle? Can sprinkles really be singular? Are they like **an** ant? Neither tasty nor ruinous?

A collection is too much, an aggregate monster. An aggression.

And what's not to like in a green-eyed monster. Ourselves. Owl selves. Our wise egos, our eye-sighted judgment. How we see others.

A green-eyed monster is a blaze. We don't see it as a constant color but one that flares, like barbecue, like fire that licks mellow marshes, moors, ceramic bowls of endless female cooking.

Cut to the jugular, Plath style with a gas jet-setter. Chose to pay very, very much. Munching on see-oh too, a languor.

Pot liquor as we say, green, as it is. Prosperity with eye please and corn braids, thank you very much.

A white bird I am not a mime. A black bird caws and is said to be ugly-sounding. Does not say what is said to it, is minor. Poe deduced this. Is why that guy freaked out and asked the wrong questions.

He hears the bird's curdling, he cuddled with the one word, loving continuity. Never left.

There was a black bird, a white ghost and a red berry. These are primordial colors, in a way. They are themes. There's light, darkness and blood. When I say blood, I mean juice. When I say juice I mean all the humors. When I say the humors I am also laughing.

It is a form of expectoration. It is a form of giving up the ghost. No one can laugh without organs, air, blood to them. That fruit harkens back to others. That fruit in that bog goes back to smoke and ruin. Smoke starts black sometimes and ends up white. Smoke stars white sometimes but falls to the earth in various colors, coloring the earth.

Red is blood including the earth's blood, lava. Water is not the earth's blood. It's its own self. If (if) it's blood of anything, it's of space. Water is the coagulation of space.

Once you add blue to the mix. Once you add a blue, well, you've opened it all up.

Once you add blueness, well. Once you add a well, well. The blueness has to shine off something, but not in a well. Out of a well, the blue shines. In a well, blue gets deeper. It departs.

Blue doesn't start in a well it ends there. It ends in a well. A well is man-made. It's a wish. One who wishes you well is a man. A woman isn't a well-wisher, she's a whoosher. When one whooshes blue one isn't talking about a well, even a big one. One is talking about something bigger though. Women don't balk at that. We woosh and shoo, which, as a wish, is practically the same.

Who/sho/however anyone knows that a blue whoosh that shines makes another color and that can be seen in cloth, in a swath, in the blanket of the swarthy, in blanket statements. In an overarching comment.

That comment is green. The green that comes from nature but isn't natural anymore. Like a well.

Well well, we say to green. That's a wish.

Upon whooshing it's we women who brought about this green color. What's on top of the earth we ask. Men often ask **who** that is.

So far, so good and bad. Most colors. Not quite a rainbow. A rainbow has several colors, that usually blend. We're focusing on the basics here. Focusing on the fundamentals, the firmament and the firm. The terra and the ephemera. We've got five and variations of those five. We've got a prime.

We've kept it neat, and that's how we know it's a lie. Nothing's that simple, nothing's that direct. Nothing's that ancient, nothing's that clear, nothings that correct. Nothing is what's missing from this halo equation of colors making a rainbow when held up to the light, the page, a magnifying glass.

Red is rid of inside and out. Shadows are rid of in light, light rid of in shadow, blue is black in a well, almost yellow out of it, frozen in the sky at a beach on a sunny day. Green is also black in the absence of light. Everything is fundamentally black without one's eyes telling you different. Until it's refracted through a lens, through a ball of flame (that is a color), until you see it vis a vis something else, it is black first and it is black last. All the other colors are subject to question, are the subject in question.

And what's the question? Who's black of course and under all that flame, what color. What is the color of de-skinned meat, raw or roasted? Who are *we*.

4.

We postulate on bile, on pus, on excretions of fat. We put it someplace else, making lemons out of lemonade, repurposing what the body doesn't use. Recalibrating what the body resists. What the truth of the matter is and how it diverges with the social order. The malleability of what the body produces in that putrid color. Do we say that it's an "ugly" color? Do we judge the things our body makes? Anything that isn't meat or bone, anything that isn't stable. Anything that can't be reigned in, is rejected. Isn't stern enough.

A woman's body is subject to change. A melanated body has contours and mystery. A body that's different from a soul is unknowable. And this variety is frightening. Shades of meaning means the devil to some. Where there is no relief from the strain of white clouds and sky, is heaven. The peaks of shadows, nooks, the fathoms and unfathomable reaches are described as hell.

Some women excrete and become the model for the rest. The rest are indicted and don't rest. Blood, milk, honey. Only one is a metaphor but the metaphor it's for is still sweet, still sticky, still sticks.

Many men say: "What makes 'em tick, these cuckoos?" "You don't ask? Cuckold" We saw what happened when we try to say there are only two sides. We tow but don't go anyplace.

Blood, milk, honey. Women releasing constantly, most women, most days. Something is going *out*.

Not every eggs works out, but every egg gets out, one way or another. Every single one. All eggs, all beings.

This is the thing about apple writing. Too easy.
This is the other thing about apples. How you like 'em?
This is the third thing about apples: they are not fruit from the middle (east—that was a typo)

There is one other thing about apples. They are akin to roses.
I could say more about apples but I won't. They can speak for themselves.

If apples are too easy, tails are… well. Don't get me started.
A tail is an extension. (Yes, like hair.) They cut them off some dogs for the same reason they have women wear heels. So we walk funny (ha-ha). The same reason they cut off horns, tusks, truss us. The same reason they skin. The same reason we wear nail paint, wear bustles. We make shit up. Tails are terrifying to those who want to contain, control. They *make* tails, lies. I say the truth is in the consumption of tails, how they're messed with.

5. (Connections, tender loins, tendrils)

[Gotta get lunch. Be back.]

There's something to be said about satiety. Some *thing*. Satiety ties something to us. Satyrs tye others to them. (Not at the shaft, nope not there.) Nookie at noon. When we talk about desire, hunger how can we not talk about it? Is it less scary in the day, during day, at the sun's height?

What is it about sunlight, digestion and satisfaction? What is it about taking things in? What is it about desire? What is it about hunger? What is it about sucking, scarfing? What is it about succubi? What is it about something sliding down the mouth either over lips or into the throat? What is it about high noon? What is it about solarium solace at a certain point? What is it about supping? What is it about the *phrase* " 'sup?" What is it about ekphrasis? What is it about echoes? What is it about coves? What is it about calling? What is it about caws? What is it about crying? What is it about tears? What is it about slathering? What is it about supine? What is it about supplication? What is it about superior anterior? What is it?

Cups, to hold in one's hand. We often think of interlacing fingers. There's something dangerous about that. The way the fingers look like clubs, little daggers. Interlacy makes a patter with the fingers jutting, evoking phalluses, torches, things that burn when you use the term "wield" next to them.

To cup is to co-exist. It is to exist in good company. Can be together "look at all the people" or side by side. They hold water and everything else. It's where cups come from. First there was cupping then there was the cup. First there was meeting then there was the meat. First there was beating, then there was the beat. First there was clothing, then there was the clothes. The mighty and the might came at the same time. They were not co-extant like cuppings though. It was one hand. The right.

First there was canoodling, then there was the candle. There was wheat, what needed to be harvested and then there was Wheatly. There was cocoa, cacao, cocoanuts, then an owl whose eye watches Wheatly's wheat and all the other plants. That was might too, and it's adjacent rhymes. What does this have to do with food? If you can't catch the consumption…well.

Neglect, sugar, cupping, cotton, rum. It's all in the mix, the batter, the beater. (see above)

A cup that's full of size is usually a triple D. I don't know if that's what she meant but that's what I'm saying. That's what Jayne Russell said, that's what Jane Mansfield said. That's what they all say, when they speak. It's not a secret. They runneth over as demimonde, as silicone, as milk. You mix one cup of one thing and one cup of another and you've got yourself a recipe, a sale. Honey.

An oyster has a cup, a flat surface, an indentation, a jewel. They wear them around the neck. Translucent, smooth, see-through. Like the cups. How else is someone going to measure? What's it hold up? What's being "measured"? What's being held? What's the hold up again?

What if you're in for something savory? What if you're waiting for fish. You try to be patient. We call girls something related to the buds. Always something depending on the taste, the date of expiration. As we descend, the less sweetly we describe them. Fibrous, fishy, salty.

Turning towards the back, we get sweet again. Slow them down. Walk a mile in her shoes. Pain for the ass.

Licking. Icing on it. Liking the lick more than the center. Liking the batter more than the end result. Liking the end more than the beginning. Liking the crust more than the insides. The dessert is more than the food, isn't it? In a way it is? In a way it looms larger like a tower.

Some say the Tower is a harbinger. Some say a multi-layered cake is decadent. Some say a tower is a sigil. Others say you should put things (letters, people, tkotskis) on the top. Some say you get through the top part to the promise in the middle. Others say you're safest at the top if something goes down. There are many connections to be made here between what's considered a confection and what's considered a construction. Something that is made. Everyone has their favorite color.

If you have something that is of ambiguous consistency where do you put it? Can it stand on it's own? Does it need to be in something? Is it an intermission? An interstate worries some people. Some folks get over it.

Oh and one other thing: Papas. (Take that where you will, sill/s/yl.) Mas papas.

"We're going to take this reed… and" You're in.

What is this thing with Black people and dairy? We are mostly allergic. We always dairying something: "like butta"/chedda/c.r.e.a.m. – we'll take a 'wassup' with dat. (Nah, not being colorstruck.) A staple? An indulgence?

At the end of summer almost all of us are a striking color.

The closest a vegan could get is an elongated vegetable.

Baby animals are safe with them. They nuzzle up.

July increases the likelihood of julienne. Etymological luck. Relaxed, anything can lie in that state.

Heating and mixing to an inordinate degree.

The punks are wariest, most vulnerable. Dissolve the fastest. Easiest to catch. They seem tough but it's all relative. There's the cooties issue but besides that, They don't resist much.

Hair is always on the fringe. Singeable.

A gravy boat. A yacht is a gravy boat.

Everything connected to pastry is Black as all get out. Quelle surprise, but true!

There's one more thing I could say about cream, cucumbers. It's too easy though so I'll leave that alone, in deference (ssf).

What's the difference between dinner and supper? Di-su, obviously. Dim-sum, not so obviously. Dimming, summer, opaquely. Dining soon phonetically. The thing is, the difference is subjective. It's deferences, as above.

I'd like to say something about hiccups here but I'd be repeating myself (bucket-of-fish).

What **she** said here is unfortunate. It isn't fortune and it isn't innate. I'll leave it there but it was a disappointment. I'll say that. (She won't.) A "a white old chat churner" after all.

Why do I get the feeling there's a feng shui undercurrent to tall of this? A black hat? Some whichwayery?

To eat is to take in **and** to bite. It's to masticate, to combine with spit, to swallow, to dissipate. To make microbial and to tend to nerves, atoms, molecules. Whatever else is there is stored or removed. It is all a very, aversion, a very utilitarian operation. Many things can, and do, go wrong though. That is the truth of the matter. That is the truth of mating. That is the truth of mater – the definition of which is to take in, raise, remove when it's too much for the body to take. Relatively speaking, this is all it is but we make such a production, such a protrusion, out of it.

So why. So why and so what? What's the big deal? What's the hullaballoo? What's all with all the vowels? What's with the opening and closing of the mouth, the grinding of teeth, the gesticulation of the tongue? The air and salivating? I'm just curious, I'm just circuitous. I'm just…

What I'm saying badly, long story long, is that there is more to this than meets the teeth and yet it's the same damn? thing. Open and such a shut case. Who are we to judge who puts what in where? It's basically the same thing we're all doing. Moving along…

Even animals, birds, plants. Even all, even out. We hustle and ham it up. We get our ____ on. (kettle, freak, et al). That's what we **all** do. Then it's done. Old Bay and bay leaf. That's pretty. Much it.

I do keep my mouth closed or put my hand over it. I do do that. I was taught. I was tuned. Subjective yes but it is.

The commonality between salad and cake are their hidden natures, their squirreling away, their mystery, their indeterminacy ("c"—custard).

What can one say about sauciness that hasn't already been said saucily? It's a consistency thing that has to do with savoriness but that's about all. The salt.

The "l" in this and all-monds is about the same to some speakers. Distinct in others. I guess this has to do with exposure, freshness, palate and the pala/cial.

The relationship between colors and foods is vague in a which-came-first way. What articulated what. Who articulated whom. Who is who and which is what. Did we see something and say that color or did we come up with a word and say that thing is it. The latter would be better, frankly. Because then the word would be waiting for the occasion. The word is in stasis. It is not a reaction.

We don't need words to react. It's biological, it's extreme. Words are an abstraction and therefore not just about the body. Food is not really just about the body. It is not strictly utilitarian. Nor are texts. They are tests of the mind, games.

Tests are a matter of tastes. Testes are a matter of mater, of mother. Truth be gold, that which came first isn't really up to debate. It begins with matter. This is concrete.

When we think of concrete we think of blood. DNA, DIY. The inextricable connotes the malleable. There is no erasure, so they say. Medical reports, genes, run. The types are singular and categorical. It runs through everything. Everything has blood even though everything isn't red. Everything has meaning even though everything isn't read. There's a reading to red. There's a red reading.

There's a red building. It's called coagulation. It's cold, coagulation. It's kohl. It's gold. All those colors together create a fruit.

It makes butter. A Black butter meaning a buttress against glare, that blackens.

Glare is a pain in the eye, despite a lack of nerve endings. Blinding is what makes us fearful. It hurts, fear does.

I think it's clear that she's saying nonce here.

Leaf that. That's what Imma do. (Amadou did and that was that. They said it was leaves later but I doubt it.) Some things blow in the wind. Blow away, are blown. I'm just saying… I'm doing that Chekhov thing for this section here.)

To add, to adorn is not superfluous, it's the essence to get at something. To take it in, to complete.

I'm going to a square place with walls, with ceilings, a bottom, with an elongation, a table to lay on. In it I will consume and be consumed. I will complete and be completed. I may have to knock a few things over. I'll be pressed. I'll get back to you. Many things will be clinking, bells weather.

Enclosed

What's a room? What's an heirloom?

To contain something. To define its size by the perimeter, parameter. A room is an act. A performer, a room does. A room is vowels, consonants, a constriction, a making, a formulation.

Rooms are temporal, a construct, an aberration, a mirage. There is a false sense, a flask, a flash of security in a room.

A room is a baby. When a baby puts baby hands over a baby face and hides you. The room are your hands over your face. A room is pretending but a room believes this.

Windows in a room are like a romantic comedy. As soon as you see them, you know the ending.

If rooms were actually rooms, why would you need another room to get a room in? Why would a room have more than one door, if it were really a room.

A room is a rum tummy. It sloshes. If it didn't why wouldn't you put rainboots into a room instead of outside the real room. Rooms are figments.

We have all been lead to believe that rooms are actual rooms when rooms are not. There are no rooms. Cells are the way we define matter but we also say cells are porous. Rooms are cells, yes even prison.

Prison is real, don't get me wrong but what are cells? Cells are structures of selfishness. Cells are shellfish. They mean different things depending on the person but they are not things in and of themselves.

Mandela made this point and reiterated it, time after time.

It is the uniformity around the cells, namely the uniforms themselves that made the rooms and cells what they are today. Give credit where credit is due. The creditors say those in cells are cretins and are getting what's due but I doubt it. No one is due cells. If not everyone is due a room to themselves, then no one is due a cell. That's just true.

Cells are uniform, a way of dressing, some say. I say some sing. That's what I say. Some cells sing despite the uniformity. Their own tones.

One can change notes in a charged way. One can chagrin. One can capture, catapult, complain.

In principle. The principal's office is a room a cell, a warning. It's "something." This is where it starts, if you're lucky: the threat of a room begins in elementary school. When you are too small to reach the door handle. When you can't reach the shelf. When the desk is eye-level, when the closet is on all fours. When you have to take a nap on a piece of square carpet in the middle of something. They tell you: that's a room. They tell you your bassinet is a room. They tell you your crib is a room. They tell you a breast is a room. They do not say a room is a womb because in the womb you are one with her and she is not anything but love to you.

Love is not a room. Love is wide open. There is safety in the outdoors.

Outdoors is where "burnt offerings" is made, according to a book that is a room. It is kept, it is a room. The burning will kill if not outdoors. The outdoors is the opposite of a room. It is free, and clear. A burnt offering is a switch a reassembling. The reorganization seems like a room but is a seam. It doesn't shut it shows where to pull potential apart.

A stone rolls over and out. The stone is a pull, the offering inside. The offerer stays out and we wait for the offer. The choosing. We must be out of our room to see it. Some say it's a freeing thing.

There is that moment in the middle. Sometimes we are too: either you're in or you're out but there is stasis. There is the stately, there is the manner. There is the manor born of matter. The material of matter in that state, in that statement is matted. It's the carpet knap. The carpet's piling.

In noir it's full of blood. Full of black blood. Full of bile. And where is that black biled blood from? It's the consumption of stuffs, it's the cannibalism of 3/5 of a meal.

A pile of naps full of blood, it is. That's what the manor is based upon. It's the foundation of the room, the objects, the food. Every noun.

Each verb reverberates, is a verse, is a reversal. How do we describe a room? By what it does. This page is an enclosure. It is an envelope(r).

Something can envelope and disperse. Is the author the addresser? Is the speaker the writer? Is the protagonist autobiographical: does owning mean being?

Am I here-ing you correctly?

There's a stage set up that projects. Is audible from the back. Chinese and Black. When we think of lions we think of manes. The largest one. The old country. The "oldest country." What do you mean "country"?

A country is a room like any other. A country is as roomy as any. A country, like a continent, is perceptual. A lion, like a liar, is based in belief. When they call Richard, Lion-hearted do they mean that he's African? How can an emblem of Africa be an emblem of Albion? The continental drift is a concept. The Suez Canal funnels it.

It's a funhouse mirror. This is glass. It bubbles in the center. It bubbles at the sides. It bubbles at the top. It makes everything a statue, statuesque.

In the room there are monuments to kings and kinds. To stiffs and the fallacy of walls. A room is romantic. I sit in a fluffy chair and pretend that it's stuffed with horsehair instead of what it's really made of: backs, piles.

Who and what to stone is a decision. What to encapsulate, to corpuscle, to make permanent. What to put one's feet upon, what to ottoman.

What to bleach is tricky, what to brighten without fading. What to make *match*.

A page is usually white, and by that we mean clean, right? (It goes with everything.) We mean open and goodness gracious. X said this, by definition. We do not say, say, bleak, blank, faded, empty. We don't say weakened state, we don't say nothing. In opposing we don't say rich, full, complete and mystery, embrace. We don't say goes with everything or **is** everything. We don't make whole rooms that color by association. We say, instead, the devil.

The scariest thing is the dick, really. For women and for men. That is the problem with demonizing, leads to castration and then what? Tying one on, that's what. Literally or figuratively. Iterations of a theme. Trading towers.

If not that then what? If not the penetration then what? If not the dick den...? Well, if not that then everything else. The corporal, embodiment, the embrace. Us. That's what I want to see. That's a room I could live in.

A fact is something to lay out. I'm saying it's plenary. Hierarchy is ideation, not factual.

Sister =/= mister is a miserly ideation, truth = be told. Happens all the time (in a way).

When they say, "we" all look alike, this is what they're saying. Difference as deference is a concept to be endorsed. I don't ad up, I'd like to think.

Harmonious is better, doesn't hinder, doesn't "hier". It receives and intones.

It doesn't cop out. It doesn't disabuse of terms that are dated. The largest number of people can't be "a" or "all". Not possible. The sense of marginalia can't also be the doorway, which is the most fortified point. The oldest can't be the least experienced, the most infantile. How do you make that work? Eyes closed, a winking acceptance, a nod.

What do we call that fine dinnerware, on which we consume, usually indoors? The apex of civility referencing "those people." There are many such contradictions in English, Englishness, French, francophilia, a continent "in quotes" and a land mass from sea to sea, defined by oceans. It's all imagination and creation. It's all. All we are, ore. All we say they are. Who do we say "we" who "they's" us?

6.

"I do." Is startling. Is a starling. Is it a "we"? or is it an apostrophe s? The difference being, the mark. Everything is a declaration: rings, utterances. Chiffon colors, chignons, veils. The veal and toasts.

It's a roast. It's jokes. An aspirant. A *whew*, small breath. Just a bit. Biting an upper lip.

Sullen, low and swole up. That could be happening. The startling, "stare decisis" means "nothing new" in this case, the many cases.

This woman with the black eye. This Black man cut down to the bone. Lead whistles and we see it, the cartilage, gristle, the fear. We talk about things: death, destruction, consuming, being locked in. What makes us sensitive, what fastens.

7.

Sometimes not to say a thing is better. It's less stressful or less dangerous. We implode, however, being entombed as we are. We are not heard.

There is the presumption of childlike innocence: should be seen only. A piece of a whole. A chip off the old. Some new little thing to play with.

Recognition is a form of association. That's how it works. A cute thing that's pejorative. There is a suppleness in the supposition but a bottom line none the more. The supposition is the *thing*. Thinging makes it a perfect fit for whatever one is supposing. Goes right in a tiny box.

When you stamp, it's quite an action. It really is something. You shape it and there is no trickle. There really isn't when you stamp, even if you're using wax, glue, blood. Nothing runs.

Stamps imply a stiffening. It makes a "thing" officially some *thing*. It's **it**. It's beyond an enveloping, this declension. It's *fixed*. It doesn't matter what it is once it's stamped. It is reduced *to* a stamp. It descends.

It hints of hickory, a blue chick too. A whiff of an embossing. That color, that taste.

It's a piano. Black and white, keys, blue, brass, percussive. Bent wood. Pliable. The violence inside. It's similarity. It pedals, has wheels and a light with specific illumination.

7.

It's bone-colored. It has feet. You can see the white, the shadow, hammers.

8.

You can count them out.

9.

He got his bell rung. He got his clock cleaned. He got knocked the fuck out. Blunt (trauma) but true. Burnt. Turnt. Like a pastry. He got blackened and then crusty. It looked like sugar on him but it was ash. All this together is what I'm saying. She and him. She is me but he is me also.

You can't, like, act like I have to be her or him. Come on, Son.

See this what happens when the epidermis, stimulated by, stimulating D, is doing something. The P we all come from. Baby 1, Maybe 0.

This will be the longest outro ever. The pianist plays a hella solo.

The packaging is the problem. The thing, the stamp, the itemization from up top. The words, used, varied and disappointing. The appointment.

There's the hunger and the mastery of that; it's satiation. The punctum is, of course, the spaces. The Sun(ra).

What about this shift between soft and metallic? The glare and the taking in? We read and do we absorb or do we bounce back? Some say: ? Mean: <

10.

So stadium, now that the ending is revealed and you coulda seen it a mile away counting pages, I'm just saying. Seering is not that hard. Searing billows, flares our nostrils and makes us make a wish.

I'm obviating here. (here) Cover me.

I put on the Ohio Players because I'm in the mood for love. The kind that comes, from honey. When we say honey, when we say heaven, I mean horns. Gabriel's bass notes.

Modern, ornate. Extra. Stein's world is an extended coda of the riff. Her ruffles a funnel from the James Brown P-funk section. I been going on rides since before I was born, not knowing where heading is and not pressed.

In the Modernist mid-section is a drum and the "2." To Picasso w/out that African hip hand is a creaky door. Cobwebbed.

You think this is a turn? What's her salon? A white place for shades of all colors, a prism. A changing disposition, a same.

"Why is a pale white not paler than blue?" Blueness is the beginning and blue is the end. There is nothing bluer. There are no other questions and no other answer.

The baby asks why why why. Black people say "because." We know truth. How early do you want to see blue, baby?

Every Black is in some sort of south. Someone sorted the south as everywhere except where they are. We didn't sort it. We didn't object it, us or them. We didn't "them" but we did "us" and have to live with that. Or die with it.

The luxury of lying is that you mean words and I mean on the ground.

The luxury of giving away is I mean stakes and you mean steaks.

The luxury of seduction is you say "come." I say, "please… please."

The luxury of saying why is there a difference is to be able to ask.

The luxury of a tribune is to speculate on what. I hear tribute, I have to give.

It's a luxury of success to question it. I have this luxury and am afraid of it. There is a luxury in not feeling afraid, guilt, impending death.

There is a luxury in saying: I'll only have one. A little. There is a luxury in growing up learning to take tiny bites. There is a luxury in making tiny pieces with a fork and saying "I've had enough."

There is a luxury in a vacancy. There is no luxury in empty.

We both discern smiles but not for the same reasons.

There is a rhythm. If we call it that we blacken it. I'm calling it that. Black. I take it. I feel you.

A life for a life. My kind of life for your kind—

No face for me. I'm a blank sleet.

It's as grey as death outside. As bleak, as pale and empty. Someone's cooking up a storm. There are ghosts that flutter between my glasses and my eyes. I see their smoke, their looming. They tease me and ask me what my fingers are doing tapping as they are. They giggle in between the paned glass and the stain.

The trees are moving but not in concert with the wind. They're waving and I get that they're saying goodbye. I wish them well. I wonder where they know I'm going.

See there are these items that flicker everywhere, solid light. Nouning like they're real or some thing. I don't believe it. I don't care what verbs are inserted. The only truth is what speaks behind, what's liquid, what's gas. If you want to know, you'll know.

Concepts and intangibles are what. What it means is what it is. We decide and that decision is not a noun it's a feeling.

The tree is felled. As it articulates angle after angel, we believe it. The spirit is leaving the bark. We sigh at stumps. We **are** stumped. The detritus of this notion: home, a place to scurry, it's slurrying blood. It's outside the color of the outtie of animals' fur, insects' web. It hides eggs. I hear little gasps as the trees' hairs stand up. The beings who live there hear the saw, recoil. Re-member.

We come back to starlings. What a pretty pretty word. Deer come in at dusk light. Nystagmus ears and tails signal before pitch clutches. Relieved before traffic quickens. This is their preoccupation and what they know.

I regret the south, what it meant to mine. I regret how much mine. How much mine gave.

There are many things China is not down with.

Change is currency. It's electric, it shorts, it shocks.

Religion is a region, is reasonable, is rigorous in its relish. And and and it is. It's an ellipsis, is elliptical, is mysterious, is mining and metered. It's merely and *miel*.

Some say it's the center. I don't know if it is but it's centrifugal. I'd go that far. I wouldn't *go* go, but I'd go *there*.

Singularity show. Now **that's** something I'd like to see. Or actually, no. Not seeing it. Anti-climactic is what you're thinking. I think it too. What's that? We only think of climate as weather and what it's not (see above). The trees are skeptical of me. They're giving me the side-branch. It's giving me shade but won't let me sit under. It calls ants.

It's not obliging just because it can't walk away. Like so many women I know, after they break down, after they try to branch out. Sends its sensors out to walk away, to walk all over you.

A canister is optimistic. That's all she wrote. Any reading she does is on a can. All she has time for as she helps the kids get ready, doesn't sleep. Tries to get caught up by reading the backs of milk cartons.

They don't put the disappeared on there. Only those who have disappeared. The unofficial ones, not the officials' ones. Still, she gets a sense of the aggregate. Her lemon tree looks at her from the outside, giving her shade. She says, who are you to judge? The tree says: I don't have a choice. She says: don't make me cut you. The tree says _____.

She reads alright. She has a can of whoop ass. The tree only has whoopsie daisy. [Fin]

Change is mercantile-ry, which is really why she can't leave, which is why she takes a switch to the kids, barking up the wrong tree. This is not a diversion of my she and black musings. If anything brings them together it's trees, amirite?

The tree is designed and is a designate, ipso facto. Whoops and a swing. A swig first. Usually how it starts – for both of them.

I have a little cake. I've got more than a little. I've got a bit of cake. More than a mouthful. Certainly enough to make a mouth water. But I'm just doing my thing. I don't want salivation on my way to the school. It's not for angels or devils this walk to the corner, crossing the street…

When I was younger they called me confections. Now that I'm older they call me or not and I'm supposed to be glad. I'm still going to school but I'm holding chalk. (Better me than them but tell the boys that. They forget I'm them, too. They draw me too.)

The amnesiacs of all hues forget themselves. I look for lights along the walkway for solace. They are not objects for me, more than nouns they are notions of safety. I hold my keys between fingers. They are the concept of clawing one's way out.

I consider myself.

I consider myself lucky. I con sider. I cons I. I, er. On. I luck. I ider and defer. I fairy. I fair well. I fare-*thee*-well. I fare. I well. All these make me nervous. Give me angst and tungsten. I don't melt down easily but I do rust. Not so much a grain of truth but mettle. No so much golden but grey. Recently isolated, I was discovered later than most.

Enough about me. Let's check on things. When are you leaving? When do I have to go? Many of us have a starched smile. Smells like lace. Looks like lattice in the teeth. Under the white, mildew. Under the doily, mold.

The molded plate is a pattern, factored in. A factotum, a farce. The solder is iron, cruel and white in its heat. Makes red whelps. A whip is quicker, cheaper, less energy. Cat o' nine tails looks like measles. Lots more going on underneath. Draconian pin pricks.

The needle point. What she collected at the beginning. Handiwork of old, hands. Smaller fingers that can do it, like a child in Malaysia right now. **Right Now.**

There's a bridge between us, across us, that spans time and people, things.

What was located in the home is now out "there." "They" do it. It's done. We have nothing to do but pick it up.

It is monopoly, mone/t/y, only, monotony.

This cloud clowns. Makes, smacks of something great. It's bigger than it appears. It's white and makes shadow. It's a contrast. The moon is white and pulls tides, drowns. In the sky but brings inside the sea.

We take laps. Laps are mirages you walk away from. They hold secrets.

Last time we saw our heroine she was looking out the window at a tree, said "fuckit" altogether. I'm just quoting, here. She's talking like someone I don't even know, not like some lady. Not like some lady in church. More like some lady who was on her way someplace and got something said to.

She got her keys did. She was asking. She was bummed out. They made her sick, en route. Uncouths.

I talked about long purples a while back. Lilacs are variations, a queered read, certainly.

They talk "funny" because you don't get the lingo. Get someone to translate. Read the signifier. Get Etheridge (again). I'm not even gonna tell you what this means: UoE'enKno. (Ursonate, glossolalia, pig latin, inside jokes. Nonaya beezwacks.)

There's more carving in a cave than in a mountain. The cave **is** a mountain and versa. Why keep digging? Vice.

Viva clink and ca-ching!! (over punctuated for greed's sake) The suffering is the echo and the extenuated dollas.

She's still looking out.

I appreciate that.

I'm constantly making my case (for my books). Constantly.

They are hard cases to make. I slip into a black robe (so-called, my skin) and remove everything else to make it.

A widow makes her claim for the center, at the sink. The tree says, yeah right. That tree is too flexible, accommodating. It's a metaphor that got her into this mess (with the washing up). There I go being an ex-pat at it.

Who says there's no pussy here? You?

Who says there's no black smoke? Not me? Been to too many clubs to deny it. Maybe now, though, it won't kill me.

Who says there's no chedda or any bread? You? Well, y'all decide so.

How's it hanging? Who says that? Men. Always measuring.

I don't write occasional poems. Exhibit ay.

There is a pecker cracker order with all that emoting and who's on first hyperventilating. Lord knows I took His time with this. And the results are up for grabs like His are.

There's a crescent moon, a sliver of light from the clouds making a cross on the tree where He's hanging. There is a sexta-star and it's all at the same fixed spot. I see it all and still don't believe it. I believe what I see but nouns are subjunctive, um, subject, er, suspect.

Why's the world's knowing attached to that one little area of the planet. To the victors go the victims' gaze, I guess. It's not exactly translucent, not exactly opaque. More like a veil one could be born with.

The ocean is encircling all things, whatever they mean. The ocean is lapping the tree...

Take care. Take care.

4. HANDHOLDING WITH SCHWITTERS

Preface to "Ursonate," Resonatæ

The germination of this sound poem started at yet another artist colony, the Millay Colony of the Arts, this time I was there as a workshop leader, in the summer of 2012. I'd selected this piece to talk about sound poetry (as well as the Stein Picasso piece). I first became acquainted with Schwitters' work in an early workshop taught by Edwin Torres in the early 1990s. Schwitters was mentioned to me again, in my first travels to northern Europe. He was just sitting around the atmosphere waiting for me to finally sit at his feet.

Many people have done wonderful interpretations of Schwitters' piece "Ursonate" including the great European sound poet Jaap Blonk and my friend to the north, Canadian poet Christian Bök. There are even more presentations on the internet.

What I did with "Resonatæ" (the title being somewhat impossible to pronounce and has a strong phonemic character to it) is to let Schwitters' poem affect me. I wanted to respond to his call in real time. Unlike the handholding with Stein, I didn't allow myself time to veer, I had to stick with Schwitters' time frame. It is also improvised and unedited unlike the other pieces (with the exception of the silences of the Cage poem).

As I've said each piece in this book presents different ways in which I'm interpreting the "assignment" of handholding, depending upon the work, its medium and my feeling about it. I guess I'm generating a template of what it can mean to handhold, what it will continue to mean for me to walk with these masters.

The audio for "Resonatæ" is available at korepress.org/TracieMorris

5. HANDHOLDING WITH CAGE

Preface to 4'33": 5'05"

In this final piece for the book, I decided to "curate" 5 spaces in silence. I was inspired, and continue to be inspired by, John Cage's work 4'33. He has said that 4'33 is about the music that is everywhere, that one simply needs to hear it.

I recorded 6 pieces, 6 spaces, and it was hard to decide which one to edit out. I'm still conflicted about it, so I added another 5 seconds as a "tag" to the 5 primary sections. I visited these places in succession and recorded them in succession. There is no manipulation of the sound. I just pressed "record." They are layered on top of each other. Besides the "tag" of 5 seconds, all 5 recordings of silence/ambience/room tone are playing at once.

The only thing I should mention is that I'd usually recorded these pieces on the first or second day that I visited the location (with the exception of the coda). I wanted a "fresh" sound before my energy settled into the room. The coda at the Brown Hotel was the place I came up with the idea for this just before I left, after a lovely conversation with the theorist and poet Jean-Michel Rabaté at the American Literature after 1900 conference in Louisville Kentucky, February 2015.

All other sounds are part of my initial introduction "to the room."

The audio for "5'05" " is available at korepress.org/TracieMorris

Photo credit Rachel Eliza Griffiths

TRACIE MORRIS is a poet, singer, critic, scholar, bandleader and actor. She holds an MFA in Poetry from Hunter College, has studied classical British acting technique at the Royal Academy of Dramatic Art in London, American acting technique at Michael Howard Studios, is an alum of Cave Canem's prestigious summer residency as well as residencies at MacDowell, Millay and Yaddo. She holds a PhD in Performance Studies from New York University. Her work has been presented at the Whitney Biennial, Ron Feldman Gallery, The New Museum, Philadelphia Museum of Art, Museum of Modern Art and Dia:Chelsea and dozens of musical recording projects. Her books include Intermission, Rhyme Scheme and handholding: 5 kinds and is co-editor of Best American Experimental Writing (2016) with Charles Bernstein. Tracie is Professor and Coordinator of the MFA program in Performance + Performance Studies at Pratt Institute, Brooklyn, New York.

Colophon

As a community of literary activists devoted to bringing forth a diversity of voices through works that meet the highest artistic standards, Kore Press publishes women's writing that deepens awareness and advances progressive social change.

Kore has been publishing the creative genius of women writers since 1993 in Tucson, Arizona, to maintain an equitable public discourse and establish a more accurate historic record.

Since its inception in 1923, *Time Magazine* has had one female editor.

Since 1948, the Pulitzer Prize for Fiction has gone to 42 men and 18 women.

42% of the members of *The New York Times* editorial board are women, 42% at *The Wall Street Journal*.

Become a literary activist and support feminist, independent publishing by purchasing books directly from the publisher, by making a tax-deductible contribution to Kore, or becoming a member of the Press. Please visit us at korepress.org.

This book's design (mostly) follows the specifications of Richard Hendel's *On Book Design*, a book whose ample margins encourage note-taking, and is a favorite of both of the designers of *handholding*.

Set in Garamond and Meta.